Constitutional Grit

Using Grit as the Catalyst for Female Equity in the C-Suite

ALSO BY DR. ANTOINETTE (TONI) FARMER-THOMPSON

"I Still Have My Tiara"

"Organizational Transformation thru Analytics," Whitepaper: ASU University Design Institute

"Institutional Effectiveness Design." Whitepaper: ASU University Design Institute

"Online Learning Effectiveness." Whitepaper: ASU University Design Institute

"Foresight Foundation for Economic Equity"

ALSO BY CHRISTINE GANNON, CEO

"Executive Women Grit: Powerful Stories of Women Who Earned the Silver Spoon"

"The Excellence Code: 7 Steps to Achieve Lasting Change"

"The Prepared Patient"

"Now What? The Problem with Military Transition"

"Hiring More Than A Hero: Five Facts to Know When Hiring Veterans"

Constitutional Grit: Using Grit as the Catalyst for Female Equity in the C-Suite © 2020. Dr. Antoinette Farmer-Thompson and Christine Gannon, CEO

Second Edition 2021

All rights reserved. This book is protected under the copyright laws of the United States of America. This book may not be copied or reprinted for commercial gain or profit.

ISBN: 978-0-578-62952-7

For worldwide distribution.
Printed in the United States of America.

Constitutional Grit

Using Grit as the Catalyst for Female Equity in the C-Suite

Dr. Antoinette (Toni) Farmer-Thompson

and

Christine Gannon, CEO

CONTENTS

Suffrage 1.0: 11

   Chapter 1: Dilemmas and Disparities in our Democracy. . . . 13
   Chapter 2: A More Perfect Union. 31
   Chapter 3: Land of the Free. 63
   Chapter 4: The Male Perspective. 85

Suffrage 2.0: 101

   Chapter 5: The Solution – Grit 103
   Chapter 6: Next-Century Grit 115
   Chapter 7: Suffrage 1.0 to Suffrage 2.0. 129
   Chapter 8: Suffrage Solutions 2.0 – From Individual
   to Executive Grit. 137
   Chapter 9: Corporate Grit and Corporate
   Social Responsibility 2.0 165

Suffrage 2.0+: 189

   Chapter 10: An Algorithm for Full Representation and
   Participation by Women. .191
   Chapter 11: Investment 2.0 – Equity Ecosystem 207
   Chapter 12: Ensuring Domestic Tranquility 235

DEDICATION

To date, the cost of equity has come at a high price for some. Continued sacrifices must be made by all, if we are to become a more perfect union in the future.

We dedicate this book to all the women and men who have and will continue to navigate this often-challenging path forward; paving the way for increased awareness and action that will result in gender parity in boardrooms and C-suites across this land.

We celebrate the centennial landmark of a woman's right to vote, secured in 1920, and we salute those who will champion equal representation and participation by women over the next 100 years, what we call "Suffrage 2.0."

FOREWORD

The year is 2020.

It has been 100 years since women earned the right to vote, *and yet* ... only 7.4 percent of Fortune 500 CEO seats are filled by women.

This book, inclusive of the 100 years following the suffrage movement, is the result of multiple years of in-depth research. What follows is designed to generate new awareness, uncover answers, dissect and correlate trends to create replicable algorithms, and ultimately, this book and the research within, reveals the need for meaningful change in public and private organizations around the world.

We have built our understanding of the current state of female equity in the C-Suite through rich meta-analysis research; reviewing, considering and sharing the wisdom of experts in gender parity and interviewing executive women and men who are organizational leaders. For convenience and reference, we have categorized our research on the following pages.

Meta-Analysis and Case Studies Representing Best Practices

- Trends, issues and the current state of women in C-Suite roles and boardrooms
- Organizational cultural perspectives and impacts
- Considerations from historical social movements
- "Grit" theory and examples

Uncommon Approaches and New Models

- Predictive analytics and algorithms for individuals and organizational change
- History of the suffrage movement
- 2020 Women on Boards ©
- Global corporate social responsibility
- Collective grit
- Principles and practices of professional athletes

Policy and Legislative Analysis and Considerations

- Business roundtable statement of purpose
- Equal pay
- Equal opportunity

- Intersectionality

Our Audience

- Male and female CEOs
- Men and women in leadership
- Women seeking C-suite opportunities
- Women entering the workforce at any age
- Current C-suite incumbents responsible for organizational culture
- Human resources professionals
- Legislators
- Policymakers
- Those interested in the movement toward equality and equity in leadership
- Current women in the workforce – entry level, managerial and those in leadership
- Academic institutions

This book seeks to reinforce the importance of female advancement by identifying the barriers to achieving gender parity and sharing leading-edge solutions to the challenges of equality in the workplace. The research collected and presented represents existing equity best practices and curates the latest research, identifies ways to replicate best-in-class gender equity within an organization and ultimately creates algorithms that harness the combined grit of individuals and organizations to create a winning formula for achieving success.

INTRODUCTION:
YEAR OF THE WOMAN

It was unprecedented. Never before had four women been voted to serve in the U.S. Senate in a single election year. It was 1992, and headline writers proclaimed the achievement as the "The Year of the Woman." And, on that Election Tuesday 1992, American voters sent more women to Congress than in any previous decade, beginning a promising period of unparalleled advances for women in political leadership. The 24 women who won election to the U.S. House of Representatives for the first time that November comprised the largest number elected to the House in any single election, and the women elected to the Senate tripled the number of women in that chamber by the start of the 103rd Congress.

As corporate women in the early 90s, we were witnessing and experiencing the beginning of what we thought was the prime of our careers, working for exceptional women leaders in our market, women like financial C-suiters Deborah Bateman and Saundra Schrock, along with other talented female leaders, who modeled successful executive leadership for us. And although we found ourselves on the 23rd floor of the Chase bank building in downtown Phoenix, we aspired to work on the 30th. The 30th floor was where the halls were longer, the furniture larger, the suites more formal and the views simply spectacular. It was the place where the word "Chief" was in the title of those who worked there, those who contributed on a meaningful management level. This was the power center, and it represented the authority, responsibility and compensation to which we had set our sights.

We regularly discussed our desire and ability to attain C suite status, and we asked ourselves what it would take and what we would need to accomplish in order to realize our career goals. We worked hard, read books, took executive leadership classes and enlisted the professional guidance of esteemed mentors and certified coaches, all in the quest to reach that suite, that floor. The challenge was, and still remains, this: We could do everything in our power to raise our ability and skill, but the culture had not evolved to align with our personal metamorphosis.

According to a study by renowned communication and political experts Michael X. Delli Carpini and EsterFuchs, in the years leading up to 1992 there had been a shift in political power due to a number of factors and doors were opening "wider for women seeking higher office."[1] This shift – as evidenced in the 1992 elections – increased interest and focus on domestic politics that was a boost to women's stature in the workplace, creating a leadership tsunami in the corporate world.

But when did this promising shift begin? Was it ignited in 1848 when the first women's rights convention was held in Seneca Falls, New York, or in 1869 when Susan B. Anthony and Elizabeth Cady Stanton founded the National Woman Suffrage Association? Or did it begin in 1918 when President Woodrow Wilson announced that women's suffrage was urgently needed as a "war measure"? "If the history of the suffrage movement were better known, we would understand that democracy for the first 150 years in America included only half of the population," says author, historian and director of the Woman Suffrage Media Project Robert Cooney. "And we would realize that this situation changed only after the enormous efforts of American citizens in what remains one of the most remarkable and successful nonviolent efforts to change ingrained social attitudes and institutions in the modern era."[2]

The pioneers of the women's suffrage movement saw voting as a constitutional right of women. We consider this research and this book to be a vital part of the ongoing movement that began 100 years ago with men and women who identified disparity and found ways to address full participation and representation for the betterment of all. What did it take? Grit. A constitutional right – equal rights – that could only be secured through constitutional grit, aka fortitude.

Consider the words of Jay Rosenzweig, a leading champion for the advancement of women in the C-suite: "Sound, visionary leadership is vital for maintaining a competitive edge. Yet when women are discriminated against and are passed over for opportunities, many of the best would-be leaders end up left behind. By promoting true equality, we can help the best leaders rise to the top."[3] Now, fast forward to the year 2020. We find that the female executive role models from our days in finance were true outliers. Today, as women who have realized and are now experiencing our earlier C-suite aspirations, we find that we, too – disappointingly so – are outliers.

Many women continue to aim high, to advance from where they are today to the C-suite – to the responsibilities and challenges of the C-suite – and/or serve in the boardroom; they pursue the opportunity, they study the obstacles, they do what is necessary to position themselves – through their grit and accomplishments – to take on the responsibilities inherent in the highest levels of executive leadership. Simultaneously, while conducting our research, we engaged in the increasingly important conversation around grit and its correlation with success. A leading psychologist, Angela Duckworth, Ph.D., captured our attention in an interview about grit – pluck and perseverance – and its role in achieving academic and career advancement.[4] Early in her career Duckworth worked as a management consultant for McKinsey & Company before leaving to pursue a career as a seventh-grade math teacher in a New York City public school. Wrote interviewer Andrea Downing Peck about Duckworth, "Watching which students worked hard and did well and which students did not, taught her that sustained passion and effort [perseverance], not intelligence or income, formed the cornerstone for future success."[5]

In her book, "Grit: The Power of Passion and Perseverance," Duckworth outlines how grit is highly predictive of achievement throughout life. Her TED Talk on the subject has been viewed by more than 14 million people and translated into 49 different languages. During that TED Talk – TEDs are powerful and highly acclaimed short presentations focused on the convergence of Technology, Entertainment and Design – Duckworth was uncertain whether grit could be built or taught. Since then, she and others have purported that grit can be cultivated. We explored this further. What if we were to start with the grit that began to develop as a child, stimulated by teachers? Nancy Bailey, Ph.D., and a special education teacher in Florida, writes about this very opportunity, noting "The grit issue goes to the heart of teaching. Good teachers encourage students to try their best."[6]

We were on to something. Take the perseverance taught at a young age through books like "The Little Engine That Could," and continue to cultivate it in young women and men, continuing this theme up to and including when they enter the workforce. How much more resilient and persevering could our next generations be? What if we consider this new pathway?

Individual grit can lead to executive grit. Executive grit can lead a corporation to corporate grit. Ultimately, corporate grit culminates in collective grit.

If grit can be cultivated, can it become a central theme in a corporation's culture, thereby accelerating individual grit specifically for the purposes of inclusivity in the C-suite and in the boardroom? We believe the answer is yes. People create culture. With grit imprinted at a young age, the culture takes on a new look, a new feel, a new promise of better.

It is our hope that the research and analysis undertaken for this book will enhance and revolutionize the conversation around workplace equality and offer a pathway forward to:

- Providing a current-state view of women in the C-suite and/or on a corporate board.

- Offering insight into the considerable opportunity that still exists for women's executive leadership progress.
- Recommending recently designed proprietary models and algorithms that create a pathway forward for consideration as a solution to the issue of gender balance in corporations seeking to close the gap.

This book seeks to reflect the energies of historical and existing movements that have been or are currently effective in creating revolutionary change (e.g., Suffrage 1.0, the Year of the Woman, corporate social responsibility, Women on Boards 2020), providing proven, leading-edge approaches to address disparities strategically and corporately, without disparaging men. History reminds us that "the suffrage movement included men as supporters and depended on men for their votes. Even when state measures were lost, the suffrage question often received tens of thousands of male votes of approval, and ultimately, a virtually all-male Senate and House had to approve the amendment, along with 36 virtually all-male state legislatures. Courageous men risked ridicule and worse to actively support women's rights."[7]

We seek to ensure the women's suffrage movement – particularly in the workplace – includes both men and women, united toward closing the gender gap and working together for equity. Multilingual strategic business advisor and change leader Anne-Maria Yritys says, "Changing culture and long-established patterns of attitudes/behaviors are among the most difficult attributes and circumstances that can be changed, in an organization or in a whole society. Respect history, embrace the moment but remember your dreams and the dreams of people … be willing to work toward making those dreams a reality – not only for yourself, but for the sake of individuals and people around you and for humanity in general."[8] To accomplish these goals, we have written "Constitutional Grit." This is a compilation of our research that includes a deeper look at the U.S. Constitution, a sacred document whose words afford protections to a country and its citizenry. When half of our country's citizens cannot fully realize these constitutional rights, we leave ourselves vulnerable morally, economically and culturally. If we continue to compromise full representation and participation of women, we disenfranchise and deprive half of the country's (and even the world's) citizens from life, liberty and the pursuit of happiness.[9]

The Women Leadership Dashboard is evidence of the work that still needs to be done to close the gender gap in America's workplace.

SUFFRAGE 1.0:

THE CURRENT STATE OF THE UNION

OBJECTIVES

Outline the current state of the union

Uncover dilemmas and disparities in our democracy

Design a more perfect union

Move forward: The land of the free

CHAPTER 1:

DILEMMAS AND DISPARITIES IN OUR DEMOCRACY

1920. A watershed year in which women earned the right to vote, but only after long decades of advocacy, awareness-building and herculean efforts that ultimately required a tremendous amount of what we call grit.

2020. One hundred years later, despite tremendous efforts to raise and advance awareness through word of mouth, public discourse and pamphleting; newspaper and journal articles, expert opinion pieces and outright advocacy; and electronic and social media accounts centering on the evolution of women to the C-suite, real progress still eludes us. The number of women in the C-suite seems to be in a perpetual state of shift – slightly up at one time, slightly down at another – but never making strides significant enough to justify a true evolution. Just this past year, hundreds of scholarly and traditional articles, as well as countless media offerings reaching millions of consumers, have addressed the limited number of women in executive leadership or holding board responsibilities. In addition, as the media titles below illustrate, some of the most notable and prestigious news entities have launched and shared their credible research with a worldwide audience. The headlines, and those of other publications, continue to spotlight the issue. Among some of the masthead treatments are these:

"The Women's Leadership Gap"
Center for American Progress – November, 2018[10]

"The Number of Female Chief Executives Is Falling"
The New York Times – May, 2018[11]"

2018's Fortune 500 companies have just 24 female CEOs"
CNBC – May, 2018[12]

"Few Women in US companies are CEOs"
Pew Research – April, 2018[13]

"Women in the Workplace"
McKinsey Study – October 2018[14]

"Where Did All the Female CEOs Go?"
Forbes – August 2018[15]

"Why It's So Important to Close the Female Leadership Gap"
Forbes – March, 2019[16]

"Implicit Bias and the Gender Leadership Gap"
Marquette University – 2019[17]

Accompanying the increased media attention on this topic was the rise in the number of powerful female characters portrayed on TV shows, such as managing partners of law firms ("Suits"), a U.S. Secretary of State ("Secretary of State"), and even the leader of one of the world's seven kingdoms ("Game of Thrones"). Individual female characters like "The Amazing Mrs. Maisel's" Suzie Myers; Julianna Marguiles' portrayal of gifted attorney Alicia Florrick in "The Good Wife"; Julia Roberts' title character in "Erin Brockovich"; "Hidden Figures," the story of three brilliant behind-the-scenes women who collectively played the lead role in one of the greatest operations in history – the launch of astronaut John Glenn into outer space – each represents the strength of female leadership and competence. Despite heightened press and attention from some of the sharpest minds in academia and media, the progress over the past few decades remains unimpressive and underwhelming, at best. Notes the Center for American Progress in a website piece titled "The Women's

Leadership Gap," "In the 1990s and 2000s, the narrowing of the gender wage gap decelerated, and the percentage of women in management jobs stagnated. And in recent years, the percentage of women in top management positions and on corporate boards has stalled."[18] In fact, as of December 2019, women held just 30 (6.0 percent) CEO positions at S&P 500 companies,[19] and in 2019 data analyzed by Price Waterhouse Cooper there was little or no upward progress in the number of female CEOs hired in several developed countries.[20]

Further, Axios reported that the share of incoming female CEOs on a global level in 2018 was less than 5 percent, down from a record high of 6 percent in 2017. The web-based news service listed "other emerging economies" at 10.3 percent for women CEOs, China at 7.7 percent, other mature economies at 5.7 percent and Western Europe at 5.4 percent. Sadly, the U.S. and northern neighbor Canada came in near the bottom at 1.1 percent, ahead of only Japan, which was at an unfathomable 0 percent.[21] These statistics present a compelling challenge and provide unique insight into culture, especially in light of a recent study from the Peterson Institute for International Economics. The institute completed a survey in 2016 with 21,980 firms from 91 countries and found that having women at the C-suite level significantly increased net margins:

"A profitable firm at which 30 percent of leaders are women could expect to add more than 1 percentage point to its net margin compared with an otherwise similar firm with no female leaders. By way of comparison, the typical profitable firm in our sample had a net profit margin of 6.4 percent, so a 1 percentage point increase represents a 15 percent boost toprofitability."[22]

Joe Carella, assistant dean at the University of Arizona's Eller College of Management has found that diverse companies benefit from increased innovation. Says Carella, "We did our own analysis of Fortune 500 companies, and we found that companies that have women in top management roles experience what we call 'innovation intensity' and produce more patents – by an average of 20 percent more than teams with only male leaders."[23]

Even with evolutionary training, education, awareness efforts and the glimpses of success that indicate women are intermittently evolving, our current research indicates the equity needle has not really advanced.

Real progress still eludes us

It is important to give further context to the current state of gender equality within executive leadership roles by providing additional statistical evidence. Specifically, we have looked at a McKinsey report," Women in the Workplace."[24] McKinsey began this study in 2015, and since that time corporate America has made minor progress improving the representation and participation of women in executive positions. Women continue to be underrepresented at every level.[25] In 2019, one McKinsey contributor offered, "Women are underrepresented at every level".[26] The simple yet discouraging assessment is all the more remarkable when one consider that women comprise 50.8 percent of the U.S. population.[27] Further, the assertion is that women held 38 percent of posted managerial positions.[28] By exploring these realities and uncovering best practices, we have developed a strategic and scientific approach to a thoughtful, progressive, accelerated and predictive methodology that can and will narrow C-suite disparity. This is a revolution within the evolution. Although many have been dedicated to the mission of achieving gender parity for years through targeted training efforts, executive education, countless awareness campaigns, and seemingly thousands of women leadership conferences, only segments of women actually reach the C-suite. Our research statistics show that even with increased activity, the needle of real change has not actually moved. Let us add perspective.

C-suite underrepresentation and participation

Fact: Women still represent only 7.4 percent of Fortune 500 CEOs.[29] That's right, only 7.4 percent.[30] Even more eye raising – and evidence of the work that lies ahead – is that a whopping 9 in 10 Americans believe the percentage is much higher. Furthermore, 40 percent of Americans think women should comprise at least half of the top executive positions in these companies.[31] The Brookings Institute: "Women's labor force participation has increased substantially in the U.S. over the second half of the 20th century, yet women in professional positions have reversed since 2000. Today, large gaps remain between men and women in employment rates, the jobs they hold, the wages they earn, and their overall economic security."[32] Entering 2020, representation of women varied by industry, but stagnation in leadership positions permeated across sectors as articulated below.

Management and professional

Women hold almost 52 percent of management and professional positions,[33] but American women lag substantially behind men in terms of their representation in leadership positions.

Legal

Women make up 45 percent of associate positions within legal firms, but only 22.7 percent of partner positions and 20 percent of equity partner roles are held by women.[34]

Medicine

Women represent 40 percent of all physicians and surgeons[41] but only 16 percent of permanent medical school deans.[35]

Academia

Women have earned the majority of doctorate degrees for eight consecutive years,[36] but account for only 32 percent of full professor and 30 percent of college president positions.[37]

Financial services

Women constitute 61 percent of accountants and auditors, 53 percent of financial managers, and 37 percent of financial analysts.[38] But, just 12.5 percent of chief financial officer roles in Fortune 500 companies are held by women.[39]

Current landscape

During the first part of 2020, a global pandemic affected almost every country and region in the world. The impacts will be felt for many years to come. This unprecedented event has exacerbated the issues of gender inequity: "Nearly 2.2 million women leaving the labor force between February and October 2020, according to a new analysis from the National Women's Law Center," reads one account workplace impact. Jasmin Tucker of the National Women's Law Center says, "There are a lot of people who [have] reached their tipping point." [40] She points to the countless women who have left the workforce since the start of the pandemic. They feel unequipped to be caregiver, worker and teacher, relative to the many physical and emotional challenges presented by the rampant coronavirus and necessary efforts to protect children and families through home schooling, online instruction and more. Claire Cain Miller, contributor a *New York Times* article, "Nearly Half of Men Say They Do Most of the Home Schooling. 3 Percent of Women Agree," says, "Even though men and women are both doing more housework and childcare than usual during the lockdown, the survey found, the results suggest they aren't dividing the work any differently or more equitably than they were before. Seventy percent of women say they're fully or mostly responsible for housework during lockdown, and 66 percent say so for child care

— roughly the same shares as in typical times."[41] It's no surprise women are saying it's inordinately more stressful and, therefore, exiting the workforce permanently.

Pre-pandemic and in recent years, the percentage of women in top management positions and on corporate boards has stalled, as reported by the Center for American Progress in a "Women's Leadership Gap"[42] article published in 2018. Some examples include:

Fortune 500

- Women hold 7.4 percent of Fortune 500 C suite seats.

- Women are only 7 percent of the top executives in Fortune 100 companies.

S&P 1500

- Women occupy 10 percent of top management positions in S&P 1500, holding 19 percent of all board seats.

Venture Capital Board Representation

Women hold only 6 percent of all venture capital board positions and lead only 9 percent of venture capital deals.[43]

The 2019 Women Matter McKinsey study illuminates critical elements of disparity surrounding hiring and promotion as it relates to professional positions and the C-suite. Notable disparities include:

- Men show as dominant in entry level positions.
- White women white and women of color show a decline in representation, level-over-level.

Further, the report outlines the legal profession as an easier path for women, but not necessarily more equitable.[44] A 2019 National Association of Women Lawyers survey of top law firms indicates that women were 20 percent equity partners, a figure increasing by only 5 percent in the last 12 years. However, very few of these firms have managing partners who are women, although 50 percent of all law school graduates are women. Not only is a 20-percent rate of women equity partners insufficient, but also lacking is the number of professional women across all industries, says the report.[45]

It is not for a lack of education. More than 50 percent of four- year college graduates are women, and 40 percent graduate from the top 10 business schools.[46] Unfortunately, improvements are not occurring fast enough in any of the high-growth segments deemed critical to the changing workforce.

Women experience disparities globally

Considered a world leader with advanced thinking regarding economics, technology and human rights – and ultimately deemed the land of opportunity – the U.S. fares poorly relative to women's representation in leadership. Internationally, the Institute for Women's Leadership has found that around the world, women hold just 24 percent of global senior leadership positions, an actual decrease from 25 percent in 2017.

The U.S. lags behind the global average at 21 percent, compared to China, where women hold 51 percent of senior leadership slots. In a study of nearly 22,000 publicly traded organizations worldwide, 60 percent have no female board members.[47]

Twenty-five percent of global businesses have no women in senior management roles. The industries lacking women among hires for leadership roles in 2017 included manufacturing, energy and mining, software and IT services, finance, real estate, corporate services and legal.[48] All over the world, the statistics are clear that there is an underrepresentation of women in the C-suite when compared with their male counterparts; women accounting for only 34.9 percent of senior managers and 16.5 percent of CEOs/heads of business in 2016-17.

In Australia, more than a third of women (38.4 percent) were managers in 2017, with men dominating senior levels of management. Nearly half of Indian women leave the workforce between junior and middle management levels, with women holding only 7 percent of senior management (CEO/managing director) in 2017, and only 20 percent of all senior roles in 2018. Although Japan has set targets for increasing the number of women in leadership positions, in 2016, private corporations had only 18.6 percent of women as section chiefs, and in 2018, just 5 percent of senior roles were held by women. Also, in 2018, Canadian women held only 28.9 percent of senior manager positions. In 2017, of the 540 C-level executives in Canada's 100 largest publicly traded corporations, women comprised only 9.4 percent.

According to Grant Thornton's 2019 rankings, 87 percent of overall global businesses reported having at least one woman in senior management, with women holding 29 percent of businesses' senior roles. Among the largest publicly listed companies in the European Union (EU-28) in 2017, only 15.8 percent of executives and 5.5 percent of CEOs were women. In the EU, 73 percent of businesses reported having at least one woman in senior management with women holding 27 percent of businesses' senior roles.[49]

Also, in the EU, France saw a three-year high (79 percent) of businesses having at least one senior woman, with 33 percent of women holding senior roles. Finland, a country with just 5.5 million people – some 315 million fewer than the U.S. – is demonstrating to the world what is possible when women have executive opportunities to fully engage. Not only did Finland elect a woman as prime minister in 2019. Prime Minister Sanna Marin, 34 at the time of her election, "is leading a coalition government of five political parties that are all led by women. All but one is a millennial."[50] It's a rarity, yet a model soon to reap social and economic benefits. In the article "Finland's Female Leadership Sweep," Korn Ferry's Helsinki general manager comments, "Among Finns, there is a certain pride that we are forerunners in this diversity".[51] Meanwhile, 75 percent of businesses in the United Kingdom list at least one female in senior management and place 22 percent of their other senior roles filled by women.

In Europe, according to Grant Thornton's 2018 rankings, 87 percent of Eastern European businesses reported having at least one woman in senior management, and 36 percent of businesses' senior roles being held by women. In the European Union, 73 percent of businesses reported having at least one woman in senior management, and 27 percent of businesses' senior roles were held by women.

Why so many statistics? Urgency.

Our intent is to create urgency around the need for change. Statistics are part of the story; measuring sticks that point to progress, status quo or regression. Sometimes daunting to read, and even more daunting to gather and record, these statistics represent the limits placed on our daughters, mothers, sisters, aunts, wives, nieces and friends. We encourage our valued readers to think of these numbers critically, not just as numbers but as mileposts in our progress, or in our lack of progress. Reflect upon them and the women they represent. This call to gender balance and female equity is personal.

The dilemma remains unresolved

1. The research is clear: Even with training, education, awareness and increased numbers in undergraduate and graduate education, the dilemma of women making real progress in C-suite positions and holding seats on boards remains. It is only in addressing these myriad disparities with individual, corporate and collective grit that we can create a revolution in the evolution of women in C-suite positions. Michael Posner, a senior contributor to *Forbes* states: "These disparities are not simply women's issues. They affect all of us. And while the way forward may require legal changes, there are huge practical benefits to

prioritizing this agenda. Studies consistently show that when leadership teams include men *and* women, fresh perspectives are generated that foster innovative approaches and solutions to problems. "By continuing to deny women access to these leadership positions, we fail to take full advantage of the formidable talents, energies and perspectives that women bring to the table and that will make our economy, our society stronger. This is a moment for men and women to make the personal and professional commitments needed for our country to become, in the words of our founders, a more perfect union."[52]

Robert Cooney, author of "Taking a New Look – The Enduring Significance of the American Woman Suffrage Movement," eloquently says, "The suffrage movement holds a particular relevance now as it has helped lead us as a country and a people to where we are today. It celebrates rights won and honors those who helped to win them. It is both an example of history suppressed and misunderstood and a lesson of history triumphant. Clearly the broader goal of women's true equality and freedom has not yet been achieved, but the victorious woman suffrage movement offers a new generation of activists a solid base on which to build the future."[53]

While not perfect, but providing an opportunity for more cultural shifting, the suffrage movement in 1920 inched us closer to a more perfect union, and a certain level of disparity has been forever dissipated. The momentum of the current movement is not strong enough to address the prediction by the Economic World Council that true gender equity will not be reached for another 200-plus years. It is insufficient to resolve the equity challenge of women in the C-suite or boardroom. As a society and as a sovereign nation, we can continue to gain traction, and with the right action become an even more perfect union for all.

The past few years of research that included longitudinal studies indicate we have the capability and capacity to accelerate this change. This is an opportunity to be more inclusive and to spotlight organizations leveraging best practices in the creation of constructive pathways for men *and* women, as well as those collective industries making meaningful strides in inclusivity. We have interviewed both men and women of different sectors to gain their perspectives and have woven their thoughts into this book. We have also taken time to review history to better understand the suffrage movement and integrate why that movement remains pivotal in our nation's journey to resolve issues of disparity.

"I think you need to make a big cultural shift," says Monica Mandelli, managing director at Kohlberg Kravis Roberts &

Co. She recalls the time she was beginning her career and an experience flying in business class: "People in first class thought I was a stewardess. Because I was there with a navy suit, they would say, 'Signorina, can you hang up my coat?'" Mandelli adds, "You need to have more women like me or others who say, 'We did it, so you can do it, too.' That, to me, is probably the most important thing to do. The second big thing is that you need to involve the men, because if we think we are going to go it alone, it's not going to happen."

In order to affect this change, we may have to reverse engineer what we already know. Cultural change requires engineering solutions that are different. The statistical challenges are well documented as is the need to employ evidence-based practices and strategies that transition us from traditional to transformational thinking, acting on intuition versus being informed by data, and committing to equity that is practiced with high fidelity. By doing so, we will avoid another 100 years of fits and starts.

We must continue forward as we analyze newly engineered solutions for cultural change and apply grit, the catalyst for C-suite equity. By doing so, we will create opportunities that will make every year the year of the woman.

CHAPTER 2:
A MORE PERFECT UNION

The effort requires a revolution in the evolution.

The 20th century arguably featured the greatest amount of social change to date. In the U.S., we were a nation solving for civil rights, labor rights, women's rights and more. Whether it was a student organization formed to confront racial discrimination or an industrial worker movement that had more than 1,800 labor strikes within a 15-year period, or the National Woman's Party securing an amendment guaranteeing women the right to vote, there has always been a group of diffusely organized people striving toward a common goal related to human society or social change. In each of the above cases, not one involved only one race, gender or group. Although each movement benefited a specific group of people, there was always essential support provided by others.

Reformative social change is often initiated at the individual level. In fact, that is what has had the greatest impact on the advancement of women in the workplace, finding more women in C-suite positions *and* appointments to the boardroom.

The informal and formal systems in place for years have created intentional networks focused on the advancement and promotion of women.

You need not be a feminist, female or even politically "woke" to appreciate the suffrage undertaking. While the subject is women's suffrage, the larger story is about democracy and how a powerless class in America won concessions and constitutional rights.

We approach this topic not as women or men but as students of American history. We see the women's suffrage movement as a topic of its own, worthy of study, opportunities to learn and grow, and rich in content. It calls to be pulled away and out from the general histories of assumptions and stale records about notable women, women of achievement, women's roles and women's stories where it the suffrage challenge has previously been hidden from view.

Leverage the past to amplify an equitable social movement

The potential for inaccuracies in history is inevitable. Award-winning author and journalist Casey Cep notes, "Impression arises only when dissent has been so flattened, arguments so distorted, and the past so tamed that it fits sedately into the terms of the present. The idea that women were always going to get the right to vote in the United States ignores the reality that they only got that right in Switzerland in 1971 and in Saudi Arabia in 2015. It also fails to explain why the right was granted to American women in 1920, as opposed to 1919 or 1918, or, perhaps more pointedly, 1776. Worse, the feeling of inevitability also conveys a sense of irreversibility, as if history always advances, and never stalls, or regresses."[54]

In a disconcerting article in the July 2019 edition of *The New Yorker*, Cep shares an accounting of the past and true realities of women's equality that is troubling. "Long before American women gained the right to vote, they lost it. Some of the first suffrage laws passed in this country stripped women of a right they had previously held. New York's voting laws, for instance, originally included mention of 'he or she' and 'his or her ballot,' but, in 1777, the state struck the female pronouns, disenfranchising its women. Massachusetts did the same thing in 1780, and New Hampshire in 1784. After the ratification of the United States Constitution, which required states to write their own election laws, the voting rights of women were revoked everywhere except for New Jersey, where apparently that very thing was legal—until 1807, when the Garden State got around to ending women's suffrage, too."[55]

Okay, wait. Women had the right to vote prior to the 1800s, and then it was taken away? This argues the idea that history will not or cannot regress. Without continued momentum, a social movement can stall, regress or cease to exist altogether.

True reality No. 1: In a 2017 report, Marsh & McLennan spotlighted the fact that "at the current rate of change, it will take 217 years to close the global economic gap between the genders – 47 years longer than projected in 2016, and 99 years longer than predicted in 2015, according to the World Economic Forum's 2017 Global Gender Gap Report."[56]

This is simply unacceptable. How can we accelerate this? It demands an intentional look at the past and a social movement with momentum.

> **"It will take 217 years to close the global economic gap between the genders."**
>
> *Marsh & McLennan, 2017*

True reality No. 2: Social movements are comprised of associations of people who connect through their shared interest in social change.

As we worked to complete final edits on this book, co-author Toni and her husband traveled to Washington, D.C., for vacation – a profound experience that would impact and validate the purpose of this book. As they toured the African

American and Smithsonian museums, Toni realized that real change would require what co-author Christine had advocated from the very beginning: a legislative mandate to accompany the movement. Toni reflected on the women's movement, realizing that the work undertaken in the production of "Constitutional Grit" would require action and real outcomes similar to the collective advocacy that highlighted our country's formation and the civil rights struggle. It requires the kind of action in which government intervention partners with an absolute corporate and collective commitment by the citizenry. The gravity of the realization was overwhelming and intense. On Sunday morning of the trip, further confirmation came while watching a documentary on Clarence Avant, the "Black Godfather" – a man who brokered deals, but more importantly, brokered equity and changed the landscape for African-American artists, producers, leaders.

Again, through the lens of the suffrage movement, it is apparent that progress is more likely to take shape when groups organize efforts and together advocate for a particular social change – a detour or different road traveled that most are passionate about but do not require the involvement or creation of formal alliances to be considered social movements. Different associations can easily work separately for common causes and still be considered part of a social movement.[108] From this very construct, we believed it important to begin with a meta-analysis – this book – which compiles and presents data, studies, opinions and facts, each assessing why women are missing from the C-suite. By doing so, we are able to demonstrate the vast amount of interest in and alignment toward leadership equality.

Ask yourself this question: If there were shared goals by these disparate groups, would they lead to greater momentum? And this question: How do we fix this collectively, coalescing our energies and research and policies? What can be learned from the past, relative to accelerating progress toward ensuring equal opportunities? What has worked to date, and where are there remaining gaps?

While there may be disagreement regarding how equal leadership should be defined and achieved, there is agreement that trends are not significantly improving or moving quickly enough. As sadly noted in the previous chapter, when looking at the leadership of the largest U.S. companies, more disconcerting numbers are revealed. Particularly alarming: as of July 2020, 37 women accounted for only 7.4 percent of Fortune 500 CEO roles.[76] Two years ago, the number was 32 women. While there is emphasis on realizing female equity in the C-suite, we must understand that the current inequality affects all of us. And, there are important practical benefits for all when an agenda is prioritized. It is our suggestion that strategies, tactics and resources are structured so as to create an equity ecosystem in which this complex network of efforts becomes a more interconnected and intentional system with shared goals and measurable outcomes. For example, Arizona State University's innovative Global Futures Lab works collaboratively toward the attainment of the United Nation's sustainability development goals (SDG). Thus, the institution has launched an effort to coordinate and integrate all work relative to SDG 5, gender equality.

Equal leadership is about a respect for diversity, working towards creating a world economy where every single human being is treated equally regardless of external attributes, socioeconomic background, or beliefs.

True reality No. 3: Progress is elusive. In 2018, Harvard Law School published an article titled, "Women in the C-Suite: The Next Frontier in Gender Diversity." In this piece are two striking findings that illustrate the elusiveness of real progress. "Despite recent advances in female board participation globally, gender diversity among top executives remains disappointingly low across all markets, with some improvement discerned in the past few years, and, second, there does not appear to be a correlation between board gender diversity and diversity in the C-Suite at the market level."[57] Cited in the article are France, Sweden, Germany, Singapore and Thailand; all of these countries have adopted progressive board diversity policies within the past few years.

However, change has not traveled upstream into the C-suite across all countries and industries. A sobering moment is experienced when one comes to realize the embeddedness and the entanglement of mindsets and manifested behaviors that must change before real progress can take place. "Thus, achieving higher rates of gender diversity in the C-Suite will require deeper cultural shifts within organizations in order to overcome potential biases and hurdles to gender diversity".[58]

Other hurdles to be jumped include the waiver/exceptions extended to private companies. Research indicates that these companies are even farther behind their publicly held brethren when it comes to gender diversification on their executive boards. Hence, 7 percent of private company board seats are held by women, versus 20 percent for public companies. Further, just two of the 200 companies – a miserly 1 percent – listed three or more women on their boards. One article references the adage "One woman is a presence, three is a voice."[59]

The analysis undertaken in the effort to create a more perfect union would be incomplete without an investigation of the Russell 3000, an important index of the 3,000 largest publicly traded U.S. stocks that serves as a benchmark of the entire U.S. stock market. The broadened view of the Russell paints an even starker picture. First, female C-suite scarcity is directly correlated with the lack of gender representation within CEO pipeline positions. Secondly, as of 2018, "Only 9 percent of top executive positions in the Russell 3000 are filled by women, which means that companies have a long way to go towards building gender equity within the top ranks where the next generation of CEOs are cultivated." However, it should be noted that the percentage of women on Russell 3000 boards increased from 19.3 percent to 20.2 percent in Q2 of 2019. Progress in pockets.

True reality No. 4: Female leadership matters. According to the Peterson Institute for International Economics, "Having female senior leaders creates less gender discrimination in recruitment, promotion and retention."[60] In a recent conversation with Pat Milligan, CEO of EDGE, the Global Business Certification for Gender Equity, she shared during a global conference for women's leadership that corporate social responsibility will soon rise to a level where young women will only work for organizations that are certified in gender equity – a meaningful demonstration of commitment in actual numbers, policies and practices. Those companies that encourage such equity will be the businesses and organizations with a better chance of hiring and keeping the most qualified talent.

Another study conducted by the S&P Global Market Intelligence Quantamental Research Team in Q4 of 2019 reports that "Firms with female CFOs are more profitable and generated excess profits of $1.8T over the study horizon. Firms with female CEOs and CFOs have produced superior stock price performance, compared to the market average. In the 24 months post-appointment, female CEOs saw a 20 percent increase in stock price momentum and female CFOs saw a 6 percent increase in profitability and 8 percent larger stock returns. These results are economically and statistically significant."[61]

Without diversity, problems arise beyond a poor retention rate, and some of those can be dire. After the financial crisis of 2008, Sallie Krawcheck, co-founder and CEO of Ellevest – a digital financial advisor for women – and the former president of the Global Wealth and Investment Management division of Bank of America – has asserted that Wall Street's issue with "groupthink" was partly to blame for the economic tumble. There was a "false comfort of agreement" among the homogeneous male leaders, she told CBS. "There was no doubt that had we had more diversity of thought, perspective, education, gender, color, the crisis would have been less severe."[62] This is a bold statement in terms of the prospect of a financial crisis potentially being mitigated if more women were integrated into executive-level decision-making and the development of solutions – in other words, a more perfect, or at the least, a more balanced union. Perhaps most illustrative of this point is a recent finding that the Fortune 500 companies with the highest percentage of women holding board positions report a 66 percent higher return on investment than those with the lowest percentage.[63]

True reality No. 5: Corporate systems must be redesigned to ensure a cultural shift where past paradigms are eradicated. In 2019, the nonprofit public policy organization Center for Economic Development produced a researched analysis that concluded, "There is no question: Women are still vastly underrepresented in the C-Suite and on corporate boards. For years — decades, in some cases — companies have invested significant time, money, and additional resources in programs designed to increase gender diversity at the top. Despite implementing diversity and inclusion (D&I) initiatives, high-potential development programs, mentoring, and leadership education programs (including ones geared specifically for women), the dearth of women in the C-Suite, in the CEO role, and on boards indicates that such programs are not sufficient."[64] Another source notes: Diversity training can help raise awareness but is unlikely to change behavior. Some research in the U.S. has found that mandatory diversity training either does not change the number of women in management positions, or actually reduces it." Said differently, while corporate America may exercise well-meaning programs and training opportunities, the overall results indicate a redesign of corporate action is necessary.

Why are some organizations thriving in the space of intentional professional development and promotional practices for women, while others are not? There are exemplars, and if companies are serious about effecting real change, they can follow the lead of the "Top 70 Companies for Executive Women" in 2020, as detailed by the National Association of Female Executives. In a recent article published by the Society for Human Resource Management, Associate Editor Kathy Gurchiek discusses the results of the NAFE survey,[65] including these findings:

- The percentage of women sitting on their companies' boards of directors increased to 32 percent, up from 30 percent in 2018.
- Female executives overseeing divisions worth more than $1 billion increased to 26 percent, up from 21 percent in 2018.
- 26 percent of the top 70 companies had female executives with P&L responsibility, up from 22 percent in 2015.

Gurchiek goes on to state that the top 10 companies from NAFE's list of 70 exhibited even more progress, including "a higher percentage of formal sponsorships in 2019 than the top 70 companies overall (80 percent versus 70 percent) and a higher percentage of female CEOs (30 percent versus 19 percent)."[66]

Another example is a health care company creating a movement in Abbot Park, Illinois. It features an employee resource group called "The Women Leaders of Abbott." This group is made up of mentoring circles of 10-15 people. Members meet with an executive leader for six to 12 months to learn profit-and-loss responsibilities, as well as ways to manage work-life balance and lead teams.[67] At New York City-based Ernst & Young, an NAFE top-70 company for six consecutive years, women exhibiting high potential are mentored through a mentors-and-sponsors program. Participants are assigned to key clients, given leadership roles and paired with people who can assist in the identification of other career opportunities. In 2017, more than one-third of EY employees who were promoted to partner, principal, executive director or director were women.[68]

Here we see companies merging effective best practices leading to an ecosystem of equity: Leadership development training, employee resource groups and mentorships and sponsorships advance to the top of the list of professional offerings that make a meaningful difference. These companies are part of the momentum and movement to affect positive change.

Adopting principles from professional sports' high-impact practices can lead to a more holistic/comprehensive and methodological approach to maximizing human development and performance. If the adage that sports are a microcosm of society is true, shouldn't society at least reflect, adopt and employ proven practices that have changed not only an industry but its workforce? Consider the approach, in sports, in which an expanded team of professionals is offered players and in some cases administrative staff to ensure or encourage maximum performance; fitness and conditioning trainers, state-of-the-art facilities, financial advisors, counselors, executive education workshops and more are all part of the employee benefits package. If we seek a return on our investment, there must be a substantial investment to ensure the best possible results. Applying such practices as those exhibited in professional sports settings to the efforts of companies engaged in the advancement of their female workforce, one McKinsey/Lean In survey report indicates that "87 percent of companies say they're highly committed to gender diversity. That is a big jump from 74 percent four years ago, and 56 percent seven years ago. However, only two percent of companies have best practices in place to support diversity in hiring and promotions—signaling a need for more action."⁶⁹

Because companies are falling short of their goals, many are asking: Why have we not seen significant results? What is not working? What can we do better? Why don't we have a balanced, unifying leadership landscape with both men and women representing the boardroom and C-suite? In addition, companies with the best record for promoting women outperformed industry revenue averages by 46 percent.

"Despite implementing diversity and inclusion (D&I) initiatives, high-potential development programs mentoring, and leadership education programs (including ones geared specifically for women), the dearth of women in the C Suite, in the CEO role, and on boards indicates that such programs are not sufficient."

The Center for Economic Development

Consider this caveat: "Traditional types of programming only scratch the surface of what it takes to help women move ahead because they address the problem on the individual employee level. Effectiveness requires a holistic approach, an equity ecosystem construct which signals corporate-wide commitment and a full integration strategy. Threaded throughout the organization's structure are embedded equity elements and expectations that drive the needed culture change stomping out stereotypes and other impediments to women's advancement. Programming, principles, and policies that hold leaders accountable in new and different ways for achieving diversity is critical; change the corporate mindset through training, conversations, storytelling, and a no-tolerance policy; include men in women's advancement and broader D&I programs; and create more inclusive mentorship and sponsorship programs to expand women's networks."[70]

Studies consistently show that when leadership teams include men and women, fresh perspectives are generated that foster innovative approaches and solutions to problems. By continuing to deny women access to these leadership positions, we fail to take full advantage of the formidable talents, energies and perspectives that women bring to the table that have the potential to make our economy and our society stronger. This is a moment for men and women to make the personal and professional commitments needed for our country to become, in the words of our founders, a more perfect union.

Imbalance and inequity

It is important to give further context to the challenges surrounding a lack of diversity in the C-suite by familiarizing ourselves with additional statistical workforce evidence. We have decided to share the statistics directly from sources to emphasize the disparities (as written) in female representation in the world/country/population and how it is juxtaposed to women's educational achievement and equal participation in leadership roles.

Women are integral to today's workforce, yet they find themselves stagnated and stalled in their executive-level career pursuits. Sustaining statistics show that women's participation in the workforce and various sectors continues to grow. Women are a force, women are contributors, women stand alongside men in many workplaces and on many levels. Women contribute to innovation and the economic well-being of this country. The information below is part of a Center for Women's Progress report titled "The Women's Leadership Gap," published in November 2018.[71]

- There are 74.6 million women in the civilian labor force.
- More than 39 percent of women work in occupations where women make up at least three-quarters of the workforce.
- Women own close to 10 million businesses, accounting for $1.4 trillion in receipts.

- Female service veterans tend to continue their service in the labor force: About 3 out of 10 serve their country as government workers.
- Women earn more than 57 percent of undergraduate degrees and 59 percent of all master's degrees.
- Women earn 48.5 percent of all law degrees and 47.5 percent of all medical degrees.
- Women earn 38 percent of Master of Business Administration and other generalist degrees and 49 percent of specialized master's degrees.
- Women make up 52.5 percent of the college-educated workforce.

According to *The Wall Street Journal* in January 2020, "Women held more U.S. jobs than men in December 2019 for the first time in nearly a decade, a development that likely reflects the future of the American workforce. The share of women on payroll exceeded men for the first time in ten years, with women holding 50.4 percent of all jobs."[72]

Stagnation – a grinding gear resulting from C-suite inequities – experienced by women in the workplace is deeply embedded in research data, producing first-level analytics comparing professional-responsibility availability with actual appointments. What is found is staggering: Across all industry sectors, inequality is apparent, illustrating slow growth or even no growth in increased representation by women in key roles/sectors. Again, these statistics are taken from an extensive report produced by the 2018 Center for Women's Progress.[73]

- Although they hold almost 52 percent of all management- and professional-level jobs, American women lag substantially behind men in terms of their representation in leadership positions.
- In the legal profession, women represent 45 percent of associates but only 22.7 percent of partners, and just 19 percent of equity partners.
- In medicine, women represent 40 percent of all physicians and surgeons, but only 16 percent of permanent medical school deans.
- In academia, women have earned the majority of doctorates for eight consecutive years, but only represent 32 percent of full professorships and 30 percent of college presidents.
- In the financial services industry, women constitute 61 percent of accountants and auditors, 53 percent of financial managers and 37 percent of financial analysts. But only 12.5 percent of chief financial officers in Fortune 500 companies are women.

In the 1990s and 2000s, the narrowing of the gender wage gap decelerated, and the percentage of women in management jobs stagnated. And, in recent years, the percentage of women in top management positions and on corporate boards has stalled. Different from career stagnation, this data suggests statistically significant career advancement is nearly nonexistent. Hence, such results remain minimally changed over time, if at all. It is also where we believe the greatest economic, social and cultural inequities exist and the most significant impact can be made. [81] Below are statistics reported by the Center for American Progress in 2018.[74]

- Women represent just 7 percent of the top executives in Fortune 100 companies.
- Women occupy only 10 percent of top management positions in S&P 1500 companies.
- Women hold just 19 percent of S&P 1500 board seats.
- Women represent 26.5 percent of executive, senior official and manager, 11 percent of top earners, and just 4.8 percent of CEOs in S&P 500 companies.
- Women represent only 6 percent of all venture capital board executives, and lead only 9 percent of venture capital deals.

- In 2014, women represented just 20 percent of executive, senior officer and management positions in U.S. high-tech industries.

From the McKinsey 2019 study, the disparities are illuminated in two of the most critical areas of opportunity: hiring and promotion. Notable disparities include:

- Entry level positions are dominated by men.
- The C-suite roles for women are stagnant from the SVP level, while the same does not hold true for white males.

An infrastructure of inequality is best illuminated at the senior-most levels of organizations, warranting heightened focus. Incongruent with a meritocratic societal structure, despite a woman's hard work and experience, it remains highly unlikely she will reach an executive level position.

As illustrated in our meta-analysis, the path to the top narrows for women and broadens for men. Women get stuck between manager and VP levels, and again between VP and senior VP. Is this due to talent deficiency? In other words, is there a smaller pool of qualified women from which to choose who will climb the hierarchical ladder? Or is the disparity the result of a lack of interest by candidates? Are there fewer prospects available, and are they unprepared? Intentional change must come through more intentional measures. Either way, it is incumbent upon corporate America to proactively address these issues. Are we ready to solve this problem?

Intentional change through innovative measures

There are numerous definitions of innovation, however, consistent in all of them is the emphasis placed on the application of good ideas and different approaches. Innovation is turning ideas into actual solutions for the betterment, whether the need is evident or not.

Therefore, sometimes innovation comes out of desperation. All evidence, as shared throughout this book, points to a fork in the road with an important question posed: Are we ready to solve this problem? America should be poised and eager: These disparities in the executive-level workplace have clearly led to a level of desperation. Men may still be viewed as default business leaders, affirming the "think manager, think male" mindset. Senior managers often apply gender stereotypes to leadership — women "take care," men "take charge." In some instances, women face the "glass cliff" – appointed to leadership positions in times of economic crisis, limiting their chances of success.84 According to TED: The Economics Daily published by the U.S. Bureau of Labor Statistics, women made up the highest share of managers in human resources occupations (70.8 percent) and social and community services (70.2 percent). The percentage of U.S.

businesses with at least one woman in senior management jumped from 69 percent in 2017 to 81 percent in 2018, but the percentage of senior roles held by women decreased from 23 percent to 21 percent.

In her research, Claire Cain Miller, another groundbreaking article titled "Women Did Everything Right. Then Work Got Greedy," in *The New York Times* says, "American women of working age are the most educated ever. Yet it's the most educated women who face the biggest gender gaps in seniority and pay."[75] There are many causes of the gap, including bias (both conscious and unconscious) and a lack of family-friendly policies. But recently, mounting evidence has led economists and sociologists to converge on a major driver – one that ostensibly has nothing to do with gender. The returns resulting from longer and less flexible work hours have greatly increased. This is particularly true in managerial jobs and what social scientists call the time-intensive professions, like finance, law and consulting – an unintentional side effect of the nation's embrace of a winner-take-all economy. It is so powerful, researchers say, that it has canceled the effect of women's educational gains.

Just as more women earned degrees, the jobs that required those degrees started paying disproportionately more to people with around-the-clock availability. At the same time, more highly educated women began to marry men with similar educations, and to have children. But parents can be on call at work only if someone is on call at home. Usually, that person is the mother.

This is not about educated women opting out of work (they are the least likely to stop working after having children, even if they move to less demanding jobs). It is about how the nature of work has changed in ways that push couples who have equal career potential to take on unequal roles. "It just so happens that in most couples, if there's a woman and a man, the woman takes the back seat. Women don't step back from work because they have rich husbands," says The Times Miller. "They have rich husbands because they step back from work."[76]

A more perfect union will exist when – as a nation, a culture and a people, not only in the corporate world but in our daily walk – we begin to see each other from a new paradigm. We must take the time to acknowledge and respect the value each of us brings, how our differences complement and enhance our environments, and appreciate the corporate/country competitive edge to be gained. This movement will take time, investment, and a willingness to see men and women not as individuals, but as one collective working to make this a land of prosperity and opportunity for all. Only then can a more perfect union be formed through upholding certain protections under our U.S. Constitution.

Equal Pay Act of 1963

Researching data for this book, we discovered new and unique information about the Equal Pay Act of 1963 that both inspired and shocked us. In short, the EPA prohibits pay discrimination based on sex, and states that men and women must be paid equally for substantially equal work performed in the same establishment. Did you know that *all* forms of compensation are included? Not only salaries, but bonuses, vacation and holiday pay, and other benefits, to name a few. Pay inequity often becomes lost in translation for lay readers or listeners, and because pay gaps are often considered political topics, ideological agendas often seep quickly into discussions. This keeps the issue festering. Gender pay inequity is a sustainability issue, not a political issue or one that should even cause division in a conversation. You may have heard about the following findings, or you may know them firsthand. One way or the other, this from "Everything You Need to Know About the Equal Pay Act" is important to consider: "History shows us although many women – women of color, immigrant women and poor and working-class women, to name but a few – have worked outside the home or been paid for their labor since the country's beginning, the world of paid work has primarily existed as part of men's 'public' sphere in the American psyche. Up until World War II, when unprecedented numbers of women entered the workforce, women were expected to exist in the 'private' sphere, performing unpaid work. Recognizing that women largely replaced male workers in war labor industry, the National War Labor Board in 1942 encouraged industry leaders to make 'adjustments which [would] equalize wage or salary rates paid to females with the rates paid to males for comparable quality and quantity of work on the same or similar operation.' More and more women entered the world of paid labor thereafter, and pay discrimination based on sex remained rampant and blatant. Women earned 59 percent of what men earned in 1963. In the early 1960s, job advertisements were listed by gender. Not surprisingly, most high-salary positions were allocated to men, and even when the same position was advertised to both sexes, a two-tiered scale ensured that male candidates would be paid more than their female counterparts."[77] In the 1960s, "a two-tiered scale ensured male candidates would be paid more than their female counterparts."[78] But based on what?

> **"Everyone thinks women should be thrilled to get crumbs. I want women to have the cake, icing, and the cherry on top, too!"**
>
> *Billie Jean King,*
> *former World No. 1 female tennis player*

In 1970, Billie Jean King, one of the world's greatest tennis players, won the Italian Open at Foro Italico. She took home $600 for the win. Her male counterpart, Ilie Nastase, earned $3,600 for winning his side of the men's draw.[118] What was that discrepancy based upon? Dan Pontefract, contributor to *Forbes* notes, "It took 36 more years until the gap finally closed. Equal prize money for both genders in any Grand Slam tennis tournament did not arrive until the 2006 French Open. Since then, whether in Australia, England, the USA or France, both men and women are entitled to the same cash prize allotment."[79] Not until 2006, continues Pontefract, "According to the American Association of University Women (AAUW), the median annual pay of all women who work full time and year-round in the USA, compared to the salary of a similar cohort of men, is 82 percent of what a man makes. A woman makes on average $45,097, and a man will take home $55,219."[80] Data from PayScale in 2019 highlight alarming new trends. For example, women with advanced degrees such as an MBA are underutilized and undercompensated for their education. Relative to every $1 a man earns, women who possess the same MBA degree earn 78 cents. The education industry is comprised of 73 percent women. Shockingly, women earn only 73 percent of what their male counterparts make in the same profession, occupying the same role.[81] If the Equal Pay Act of 1963 "prohibits pay discrimination based on sex and states that men and women must be paid equally for substantially equal work performed" why, in 2020, are we still seeing this disparity in our country?

"Relative to every $1 a man earns, women who possess the same MBA degree earn 78 cents."

Dan Pontefract, journalist and author

In 2016, the Economic Policy Institute released a guide to the gender wage gap that demonstrated the gap grew greater as women earned more. Today, the loss in lifetime earnings is $530,000 for the average woman and $800,000 for college-educated women. Gould, Schieder and Geier, writing for the Economic Policy Institute, have noted, "Over the past three and a half decades, substantial progress has been made to narrow the pay gap. Women's wages are now significantly closer to men's, but in recent years, that progress has stalled. From 1979 to the early 1990s, the ratio of women's median hourly earnings to men's median hourly earnings grew partly because women made disproportionate gains in education and labor force participation. After that, convergence slowed, and over the past two decades, it has stalled. According to the most recent data, as of 2015, women's hourly wages are 82.7 percent of men's hourly wages at the median, with the median woman paid an hourly wage of $15.67, compared with $18.94 for men."[82] Other findings from the Economic Policy Institute report include the fact that women who take time out from the labor force pay a high price that is increasing; the provision of paid leave and affordable child care are critical to women joining the labor force and narrowing the gender wage gap, and strengthening enforcement of Title IX and EEO policies is also crucial to narrowing the gender wage gap.

In sports, the gender pay gap continues despite years of advocating on behalf of women athletes. Scott Davis published an article in the Business Insider stating, "The prize money for this year's (2019) women's soccer World Cup is $30 million across all 24 teams, double the $15 million it was in 2015, but still a sliver (7.5 percent) of the $400 million in prize money for the 2018 men's World Cup in Russia. And the total prize money for the men's teams playing at the 2022

World Cup in Qatar will rise to $440 million. According to the Australian players' union, at this rate, it will take until 2039 for pay to become equal."[83]

What is *this* gap based on? We continue to ask the question, and the resulting silence defines the existing issue. It will take until 2039 for the World Cup gap to shrink and 257 years for equal pay[84] in corporations, with even more disparity in diverse women populations. At what point do we make the shift from discussion and research to real, measurable, accountable action? It is up to us to make this happen.

Why is equal pay so important? A 2016 study highlighted what many fail to recognize about pay inequity: It is more than just an economic issue. Columbia University (Platt, Prins, Bates & Keyes, 2016) puts forth a possible new explanation for the higher rates of depression and anxiety seen in working women — and women in general — compared with rates in their male peers. The study found that women were 1.96 times more likely to experience depression and 2.5 times more likely to experience anxiety than men.[84] These incidences leveled out when women were compensated at the level of their male counterpoints. It seems women internalize the disparity and attribute it to the lack of their personal value or worth rather than of the unfair and biased institutional practices that are at the root of the problem. Researcher Platt and his colleagues interpret gender-related income disparities as suggestive of women being undervalued and as a potential proxy for other forms of bias, such as denying promotions on the basis of gender. There is substantial evidence that discrimination — including sexual harassment and workplace aggression — is associated with depression, anxiety, symptoms of post-traumatic stress disorder and substance use.[85] We can and must do better in our society, in the workplace and in our culture.

CHAPTER 3:

LAND OF THE FREE

Real Truths and Common Misperceptions

With the economic case for diversity having been made, why are we still seeing stagnation in the advancement of women in the C-suite? McKinsey and Deloitte, two powerhouses of workforce research and solutions, have demonstrated confirmed advantages relative to increased net profits and cash flow when women are at the helm. In recent reports, organizations are asking, "How do we build an organization that better identifies and leverages high-potential female leaders, and also works to ensure more women succeed in the future?" In a recent article published by Linkage, the authors point to the need for a strong framework. "The situation for many organizations looking to achieve gender parity is comparable to trying to cook a gourmet meal without a proven recipe or possibly even without ingredients."[86] What, then, are the ingredients and the recipe? Several organizations have solved the problem, and many are beginning to document their roadmap.

Research shows that change begins at all levels, and possibly most importantly with intentional and inclusive leadership from the top, positioning women to gain the experience needed to work in the C-suite. In order to develop the pipeline of potential women for C-suite inclusion, executives must close the gender gap at the executive leadership level and support women early in their careers with sponsors, access to profit-and-loss roles, and the opportunity to serve as an outside director on a corporate board. How do we close this gender gap? Only with individual, corporate and collective grit, which begins by facing our misperceptions. Trading past misperceptions for today's truths can accelerate change.

Dispelling some of the most egregious perceptions is a *Harvard Business Review* survey titled "We Interviewed 57 Female CEOs to Find Out How More Women Can Get to the Top," written to provide insight into common misperceptions and real truths relative to women leadership that may help advance the thinking of those responsible for selecting CEOs, CFOs, CIOs, etc. This was no cursory, superficial survey. Six perceptions were included in the study:[87]

Perception No. 1: C-suite sooner? Women are ready

Women are said to be stifled and therefore delayed in attaining the top jobs because they are often in support roles, required to prove themselves 10 times over before given additional opportunities, thus extending their tenure and lengthening their runway while shortening their time in leadership positions. Research indicates that women often leave companies for this very reason, as noted in another *Harvard Business Review* piece, "How We Closed the Gap Between Men's and Women's Retention Rates."[88] Researchers found that "gender disparities in our senior cohorts are not completely explained by traditional workplace concerns, such as work-life balance, maternity leave, unequal pay, and differential ambitions. We have identified a very different explanation, which is just as critical: the quality of the day-to-day apprenticeship experience." Earlier in this book, we noted that the preparation element for women to assume C-suite roles is limited. Are women ready? Most often, yes. Are they adequately prepared? Not quite.

Companies may want to institute targeted retention analysis, then corresponding programming for women at key levels to create a variety of opportunities. As mentioned in the previous chapter, representation/participation gaps widen at higher managerial levels. Looking at the data, it is obvious women are stuck in or between, often when they reach a management level, continuing up through VP levels. McKinsey & Lean In label this lack of advancement the "broken rung" theory. It is when women's progress is stunted, keeping women from reaching the top of the ladder. Many work the remainder of their career at these levels. If perpetuated over the next 10 to 50 years, this is a much more economically, socially, and culturally dangerous and desperate circumstance.

How then do we get women unstuck? We agree with the broken rung analogy and would liken it to a medical metaphor. Consider this: When blood flow is decreased, and sticky substances called clotting factors cause blood cells to clump together, a blood clot is formed. Blood contains plasmin, an enzyme that acts to dissolve certain blood clots. Clots cause heightened medical risks and threats and, therefore, require immediate treatment. Most commonly used to address this issue are anticoagulants, also called blood thinners, that help to prevent blood clots from forming. Similarly, organizations must understand that the seriousness of their "career-clot" conditions requires anticoagulant actions.

We propose companies start with a comprehensive assessment. This assessment can provide an understanding as to the percentage of women compared with men within each leadership level, as well as their tenure with the company, pay, education, performance and time in a leadership position. Leaders should be asking, "Are women stuck in my organization? If so, where and why? Why haven't we promoted her? Does she have feedback? Is there a development pathway in place?"

> Are women ready? Most often, yes.

Perception No. 2: Business results and positive impacts are key drivers for women

In the aforementioned *Harvard Business Review's* "We Interviewed 57 Female CEO's," authors Stevenson and Orr note, "Drive in high-achieving women manifests differently from the top-performing, predominantly male CEO benchmark group, despite their capabilities showing as almost identical on other fronts."[89] City of Phoenix Chief of Police Jeri Williams is one such example. A perfect blend of an outcomes-driven leader and friend, Chief Williams, say her colleagues, is someone who gives everyone the same attention and respect, making everyone feel valued, resulting in an extraordinary connection between rank and file and chief. Further, people (community and colleagues) are more relaxed, able to offer their best ideas and their best selves. One employee shared "When seeing the uniform, there can be admiration or admonition, also assumptions that she will act a certain way." Williams proudly states, "I am 52 years old," and says she "will never forget where I came from." These are descriptors that not only make Chief Williams approachable, but impactful. From our conversation, it was clear that others (men) are more formal in their interactions, however the chief seeks to create personal connections whenever and wherever she can.

Chief Williams comments, "I believe in the concept first stated in Malcolm Gladwell's book 'Outliers,' which says that anyone can master a skill with 10,000 hours of practice. I was never afraid to put in the time to master anything I was inspired to master. That being said, these are things that are attainable and not pie in the sky. I could never train enough hours to be a superstar basketball player due to my 5'-5" height. I showed up to every meeting, I pursued professional development and got my MBA, I pushed myself hard. I had a reason to never want to repeat the first part of my life, my childhood. I also volunteered for every special assignment or project. I loved learning new things and building my skill set. It was a passion or obsession, maybe both. I wanted something more."

Another interviewee for this book, retired Lt. Col. Sharon Preszler – the first female fighter pilot in U.S. military history – says, "I did not do things differently, as much as I was different. Because I was different and the first woman venturing into this particular man's world, I was forced to be an instrument of cultural transformation in the USAF (Air Force) fighter community. It was a lot of pressure knowing that you could never blend in or 'fly under the radar.' People were always watching me, some hoping I would succeed and some hoping I would fail. But either way, I knew they were watching my progress. I also felt early on that the hopes of all women who would ever want to fly fighters rested on my shoulders. That is a lot to take on in an already intense and sometimes hostile training environment, and it took me a while to learn to deal with the additional pressure."

Women are driven by achieving and making a positive impact in their culture and industry. In varied studies we have researched and noted throughout this book, creating a positive culture is listed as one of these women's most important accomplishments. Social responsibility and embeddedness are tenets of corporate responsibility, critical to building trust with clients and the community at large. Organizations may want to consider setting a benchmark that aligns with corporate interest and also the strength of women; a strength that may be imperceptible yet inspiring, to others. The women we interviewed articulated deeper meanings that manifested in their personal pursuits and achievement.

> "I didn't do things differently, as much as I was different. Because I was different and the first woman venturing into this particular man's world, I was forced to be an instrument of cultural transformation in the USAF fighter community."
>
> *Lt. Col (Ret.) Sharon Preszler, first female fighter in U.S. military history*

Perception No. 3: Specific traits are essential to women's success and are in short supply

Throughout the *Harvard Business Review's* study of female CEO assessments, a combination of four traits and competencies emerged as key to their success: courage, risk-taking, resilience and managing ambiguity. Because of the alleged short supply of women with these success traits, it is even more critical to develop succession pipelines filled with women who possess these specific traits. Whether or not they are ready becomes of critical importance for women who possess these four traits. When our "Constitutional Grit" interviewees were asked to share which of these "grit-like" traits they most possessed, their answers were both varied and interesting. Here are just a few of them:

"Perhaps starting a nonprofit agency (Gabriel's Angels) was my grittiest move to date. Risk is an element of grit. A nonprofit startup success rate mirrors the for-profit sector in that approximately only 3 percent will make it to the fifth year.

"It took an immense amount of courage to start from scratch in a niche (pet therapy for abused and neglected children) that did not exist eighteen years ago. I did not have any model I could utilize for success. I had to create momentum to educate people on this new concept. People had heard about therapy dogs in hospitals and nursing homes but not healing children in crisis. It also took an immense amount of endurance to keep my eye on the long-term vision while growing Gabriel's Angels."

Pam Gaber, founder and CEO, Gabriel's Angels

"Courage, mostly ... Being the new girl in 10 different schools and 13 years in the military took my natural courage to new heights. It definitely took courage and follow-through to make it through F-16 training and then move with my husband to Germany to meet my new squadron, a squadron that I knew some of them didn't want me in. Courage and resilience which adds purpose and passion to 'everyday work' which requires you to be vulnerable, willing to fail (and) causing you to believe so strongly in something.

"I can look back and see things from my childhood that toughened me up, but nothing that truly prepared me for what I faced as the Air Force's instrument of change. I think a lot of it comes from how you are raised. Did your parents encourage you to take risks? Were you raised to believe it is better to have tried and failed than never to try at all? Or were you raised in a sheltered and protected manner, so you never get hurt but you also aren't challenged and don't build that confidence or resiliency?

"I believe most of the time you don't know what you can handle in terms of challenges until you are in the middle of them. Courage allows you to accept the challenge. Then, you use your prior experiences and those characteristics of resiliency and being achievement-oriented, and you focus on what you want to accomplish."

*Sharon Preszler,
U.S. Air Force Lt. Col. (Ret.)*

Executive training professional Cheryl Levick reflected upon this statistic: "Female CEOs scored significantly higher – in the 70th percentile – than the benchmark for humility, which was in the 55th percentile. However, compared with the predominantly male CEO benchmark, the women scored lower on confidence, measured as a function of belief in whether they were in complete control of events and outcomes that define destiny." Here is what she says about the above:

"Things are improving, as demonstrated by [the fact that] the last three placements in assistant athletic director roles throughout U.S. universities were female, and it was my pleasure to mentor them and be with them every step of the way. Critical are confidence and competence. Yes, many have the degrees and the necessary experience, however you only have 3-5 seconds to demonstrate an air of confidence."

Confidence is what Lisa Stevens Anderson, CEO Equality Health, another "Constitutional Grit" interviewee, has worked at the hardest. She says, "We think we have to be perfect, but we do not. There is always going to be someone better at something." She became very adept at not letting anything get in her way, and at the lowest points, remembers that "everything can be solved with sleep … the sun does come back up. This gives a totally different perspective and you again realize that you can control your own destiny."

Mayo Clinic Professor of Radiology Oncology Dr. Michelle Halyard says, "As a young black lady, you have to find your identity in other ways, however things change as you get older. Attending a historically black college or university was helpful, as there was no one judging whether or not you are good enough, and more importantly, there is no self-doubt, helping to build a sense of self confidence and getting a tremendous start."

Perception No. 4: Women harness the power of experts and teams

In her article for *Forbes*, Shelley Zalis, founder and CEO of The Female Quotient, points out, "The path to leadership is about learning, growing and evolving."[90] Catherine Blackmore, global vice president for SaaS Customer Success at Oracle, says, "Unfortunately, many women may hang out with people who see them [for] far less than they are or spend time with people who see them at their current level, because it feels comfortable. But if you surround yourself with those people who push you beyond your current capabilities, you will be more likely to stretch yourself. It's uncomfortable, but that's how we can truly grow and rise up into top leadership positions."[91]

The authors of this book can attest to the fact that reaching into your professional network is critical in attaining an executive role and C-suite status. The perception that a woman, or a man, can go it alone and achieve this level of success if a falsehood. We have each benefited from networking with experts and collaborating with teams throughout our careers, and we have found both experiences extremely beneficial in opening pathways for women to rise to new levels.

Perception No. 5: Dream bigger – C-suite or executive status doesn't appear in many women's vision of their career

As women realize they have more to learn, particularly in taking on a new role, they are more inclined to ask for help and give credit to others for their success. Too often, they forget to create a vision for themselves that includes being CEO or joining a corporate board.

"It was important that I believed in myself – the belief that I was stronger than the situation and the belief in my ability to overcome it. If it is going to be, it's up to me! Wallowing in low points is simply unproductive. Also, the low points in our life are the catalyst for the next high point, as life is not a vertical line of events," says Gabriel's Angels founder and CEO Gaber.

People Matters, an HR media platform founded in 2009 to foster ideas between HR-related professionals, cites the study "Women in Corporate Boardrooms," a survey of 500 women leaders and 1,000 women professionals across various industries: "When asked about their interest in becoming CEO, 71 percent of women respondents expressed an interest, while 29 percent did not have a desire to become CEO of their existing company. Then, when asked about the possibilities of it happening, only 10 percent said they had a high probability of becoming the CEO. About 44 percent said they had a very marginal chance of becoming a CEO. My advice for women who want to rise up into leadership is to stop asking yourself if you can. Doubt is killer for action and promotion," says Corporate Vice President, Corporate Strategy, Partnerships and Business Development at Nissan Motor Co., Ltd., Catherine Perez. "If it is in your mind, it will enter others' minds. Do not question yourself. Start walking, and the path will create itself under your feet."[92]

Would more women see themselves in these leadership positions if they were to see others in them? Part of our research included qualitative conversations with young women, ranging from college sophomores to those in their late twenties. Perhaps most compelling was the conversation with Shayla, a college sophomore, who candidly shared that many young women in college do not realize the current struggle with equity in the C-suite or boardroom. In fact, many are unaware of what a C-suite is. Shayla had recently won a research competition and secured a competitive internship with a prominent, innovative consulting firm solving for significant societal issues such as healthcare. It is uncustomary to offer sophomores such positions, however Shayla's regional leader saw her talent and potential, so took the time to serve as an involved mentor. Without this mentorship, Shayla says she would not have her strong leadership aspirations. Thanks to the involvement and support from her female mentor, Shayla now sees COO, CFO or even CEO in her future.

Perception No. 6: Launch pad for female CEOs – Backgrounds in STEM (Science, Technology, Engineering, Math), business, finance or economics

Again, from the Harvard Business Review: "Forty percent of female CEOs started out with some technical expertise in STEM, and close to 20 percent started with a background in business, finance or economics." This statement alone provides tremendous insight into a potential area of focus in the shifting paradigm. Statistics tell the story: Eleven percent of CFOs across industries are women, according to a survey of top 1,000 U.S. companies by executive recruitment firm Korn Ferry. The survey was conducted in mid-December 2017, and the figure was down from 12 percent in 2016. Retail was the industry with the most female CFOs, 19 percent, followed by consumer goods at 15 percent. Finance and health care were tied at 8 percent. The executive search firm noted that while the percentage of female CFOs dipped slightly in 2017, it was seeing a positive trend of women being internally promoted to CFO.[93]

A gentle reminder: More than 50 percent of four-year college graduates are women, and 40 percent of graduates from top-10 business schools are women. If companies are not recruiting women in STEM leadership or finance positions, are they truly serious about C-suite diversity?

> **"While women make up half of the total workforce in the U.S., they only make up 29 percent of the science and engineering workforce, according to the National Girls Collaborative Project. Yet, women constitute 50.3 percent of science and engineering degrees. Somewhere between their college education and their career, women are leaving STEM.**
>
> *Spaces 4 Learning, "Spotlight on Women in STEM Leadership"*

National Geographic leads a 2019 article, "The Best & Worst Countries to be a Woman," with the following statement: "No country has it all, but some places are better than others."[94] The Women, Peace & Security Index measures women's inclusion in society, their sense of security and their exposure to discrimination. Highlighted in an article published by the organization is Gulalar Ismail, a Pakistani woman activist who escaped to New York so that she might remain alive. She has no formal education and is illiterate, but very smart – smart enough to realize the importance of data in conveying her circumstance. She did so by placing 25 straight lines on a piece of paper, each one indicating the number of times she was sexually harassed by security forces, creating a record of abuse. That is the purpose of sharing and the power of this data – "the ability to track information, to collect it, to have data readily available … it [data] has the power to embarrass, to highlight success, to spark media coverages, and to pinpoint where change is needed."[95] Ranking 167 countries, a Georgetown University Institute for Women, Peace & Security study ranked the U.S. 19 of 167. High marks for women's schooling, but lower rating due to inclusion inhibitors.

While progress continues to be made in increasing the number of women on boards to 20 percent, that progress cannot be correlated to women gaining seats in top executive leadership positions. The chart below demonstrates this well, as the highest representation of women on boards is held by Belgium, however only 10 percent of their corporations are headed by a woman. Belgium holds the third-highest number of women on boards among countries surveyed, and executive women leader representation sits at 32 percent, an overall ranking of No. 4.

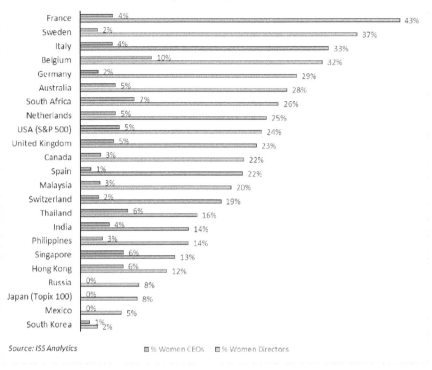

Further work conducted by the World Economic Forum, culminating in its report, "Global Gender Gap Report 2020," provides tremendous insight through the Global Gender Gap Index score. The score was calculated using four key measurements: economic participation and opportunity, educational attainment, health and survival, and political empowerment. The methodological construct has not changed since its inception in 2006, providing effective comparative points for 153 countries. Highlights from 2020 include:

- Globally, the distance to parity is 68.6 percent, leaving an average gender gap of 31.4 percent.
- All but 39 countries (of 149) increased their scores, although improvement, there is not sufficient progress
- Of the four measuring categories, the greatest disparity resides in the area of political empowerment (24.7 percent), then economic participation and opportunity (57.8 percent). The other two factors scored in the mid-90th percentile.
- Of the 35,127 political seats available globally, only 25 percent are held by women — 21 percent of ministerial seats. In 85 of the 153 countries, there has not yet been a female head of state.
- While progress has been made in closing the educational attainment gap, there is still a population of young girls without access — globally, 10 percent of girls between the ages of 15-24 are illiterate. This becomes even more concerning, given the next finding regarding professions of the future.
- "Based on data from the LinkedIn platform, women are underrepresented in six of the eight micro-clusters with the highest employment growth rate."[102]

- "At the slow speed experienced over the period 2006-2020, it will take 257 years to close the gap globally. North America 151, 163 years in East Asia/Pacific, 54 years in Western Europe, 59 years in Latin America and the Caribbean, 71.5 in South Asia, 140 in the Middle East, 95 in Sub-Saharan Africa, and 107 years in Eastern Europe/Central Asia."[96]

Progress is thought to be slow and uneven across and within the various continents. Some of these projections are puzzling, given how economically and politically advanced some of the countries are said to be.

When there was just one woman at the C-suite table, women were 49 percent more likely to have their judgment questioned than men.[104]

"Women in the Workplace, McKinsey & Co., 2020

CHAPTER 4:
THE MALE PERSPECTIVE

Just as men were a critical part of the suffrage efforts of a hundred years ago, the next-century 2.0 suffrage movement also requires next-level grit for men. Let's address the question many overtly ask or are covertly considering: How do men feel about women either not rising to the C-suite or, conversely, being given more opportunity to attain the coveted senior leadership roles women seek within their companies?

The Center for Economic Development reports "Nearly 50 percent of men think women are well represented in leadership, but research shows only one in 10 senior leaders is female. Companies need to make men part of the solution by educating them on the challenges that women face and providing the resources to create gender diversity."[97]

"Companies need to make men part of the solution by educating them on the challenges that women face and providing the resources to create gender diversity."

> *"Filling the Pipeline: AdvancingMore Women into the C Suite and on Corporate Boards," Committee for Economic Development, 2019r recruiter t appreciated, and our readers are encouraged to ent this in regular content format. Stevet in a block format.*

It is no secret that men hold most of the powerful positions in corporate America, especially when it comes to venture capital funding. So, we need to support women in every way possible. Simply giving positive feedback and recognition can go a long way. Most people do not change or willingly go along with change simply because "change is the right thing to do." They do it if there is an important reason to change. Generally, businesses do not change their corporate cultures to improve the retention of their female workforce because it is a nice thing to do. They do it if there is a compelling business reason that can increase their bottom line.

In his article, "Three Ways Men Can Help Close the Gender Gap," Joshua Lee says, "A more diverse workplace is proven to generate better ideas and outcomes. Bottom line, the time is now to achieve gender diversity if you want an innovative, profitable business."[98] McKinsey & Co. recently conducted a research study consisting of 132 global companies, surveying 34,000 men and women regarding their experiences at work. The findings provided an alarming and a surprising data point: "The disparity begins at entry level, where men are 30 percent more likely than women to be promoted to management roles. It continues throughout careers, as men move up the ladder in larger numbers and make up the lion's share of outside hires."[99]

Nikki Waller of *The Wall Street Journal* says, "Data shows that men win more promotions, more challenging assignments and more access to top leaders than women do. Men are more likely than women to feel confident they are in route to an executive role and feel more strongly that their employer rewards merit."[100] It is no surprise that men view merit as the basis for promotion.

A man's view of women in CEO seats also matters, according to Andromachi Athanasopoulou, assistant professor of organizational behavior at Queen Mary University of London and associate fellow in executive education at the University of Oxford. Males continue to dominate senior leadership roles and coveted CEO spots in corporate America. "Men would say things like, 'You still have to maintain your femininity,'"

Athanasopoulou says. "For a woman, they see if they are too pushy, they don't get things done. Men don't accept that. So, women tend to feel they have to span both demands of being assertive, or being a leader, and yet being empathetic and transformational in their leadership style."[101]

Dave Adams is president and CEO CU Solutions Group. In 2018, he took time to reflect on his career in banking and shared his insights with his organization's publication, "Credit Union Insights." He has allowed us to reprint his article in full, which appears below.

"A Male Perspective in Finance," Dave Adams

"As we age personally and professionally, I think we all ask the question, 'If I had it to do all over again, what would I change?' As a 60-year-old white male executive, one thing that I would have done more effectively is mentor both men and women within my sphere of influence. Now, like with any introspective assessment, I have to say that I haven't failed, I just could have done better. But despite my shortcomings in this area, I can bring awareness to the topic and use my remaining years to make a meaningful difference.

"A good friend of mine, who happens to be a hard-driving, tenacious young leader, helped me to see one of my flaws. She never referred to me. She just described her journey and perspective and, unfortunately, in far too many ways, I saw myself in her examples of male ignorance in the area of mentoring. As she pointed out, as a woman, she noticed that when power lunches or small golf outings were organized, the guys often seemed to exclude women. These men didn't mean to be exclusive, but they migrated to the 'good old boy' outings, as opposed to being inclusive.

"As subtle as her examples were, I realized, much to my dismay, that I had been guilty of some of those practices. Whether it was filling a golf foursome, scheduling lunch meetings or while attending after-hour cocktail events or dinner meetings, I often favored male team members. What was once an unconscious action has become noticeably clear. Now I look for opportunities of inclusivity in these types of social settings. And of course, this occurs with all affinity groups such as female executives, young professionals, certain specialized employees or demographic groups. The message is this: Inclusive mentoring is not just a gender issue; it should be required of all executives and apply to all types of diversity. For all leaders … we need to work harder to institutionalize inclusion in boardrooms, executive teams and individual departments.

"It's well known that in corporate America, 95 percent of the Fortune 500 companies are led by men. General Motors' CEO Mary Barra is an exception to this trend. In a male-dominated auto industry, she has overseen one of the most remarkable corporate turnarounds in U.S. history. Mrs. Barra is an incredibly respected leader who has fought her way through the power structure to achieve the top status at GM. As a former HR executive at GM, Barra brought amazing insight and the power of simplicity to the company's dress code by reducing it to two words, 'dress appropriately.'

"Diversity challenges the status quo and brings fresh perspective that drives innovation and culture enhancements. "In his book, 'Why Women? The Leadership Imperative to Advancing Women and Engaging Men,' author Jeffery Tobias Halter suggests that 'engaging men as champions and advocates who recognize the value of women is the cornerstone of organizational success. They must be leaders who get it and walk the talk every day in their actions and communications.'

"My mother raised me and my three brothers alone after my father died in a small plane crash in 1961. She had only a high school education and worked mostly minimum wage jobs. She faced discrimination and sexual harassment in the small company she worked for. She was and is the toughest person I have ever known. What she taught me was tremendous respect for the unique attributes of female leaders.

"Let's face it, we are different. And it is precisely those differences that should require us to seek gender and ethnic diversity at all levels of our organizations and an absence of discrimination of any kind."

"Credit Union Insights," Dave Adams, president and CEO, CU Solutions Group

Creating and fostering a culture of inclusion and respect, along with zero tolerance for discrimination is critical for any company's brand and effectiveness. "I suggest that there are five things that every male and female executive should consider as a self-assessment and resolve to broaden awareness and be more inclusive in mentoring, especially as it relates to gender inclusion.

"First, get rid of the excuses. "Consciously or subconsciously, we all have our excuses for maintaining the status quo. Get rid of them. This is not going to create a culture of reverse discrimination. It is about inclusion and giving everyone a fair shot. And no matter how good you think you or your organization are doing, you can and should do better. Gender and ethnic diversity bring more innovation and creativity and greater alignment with the members you serve. It also strengthens your corporate brand internally and externally. And it's the right thing to do.

"Second, do an honest inventory of your behavior.

"Every executive should do a complete self-assessment. It isn't enough to be tolerant or to not discriminate. Take a look at your unconscious bias. The real question is, do you look for opportunities to proactively mentor both men and women in your organization? And do you do so with equal favor to men and women? Get rid of all exclusionary tendencies that favor men or women. Realize that you have a responsibility to mentor equally and fairly.

"Third, conduct an objective review of your organization's practices with regard to gender inclusion and pay equity.

"After attending a National CU Roundtable meeting where gender inclusion was showcased, I came back to the office and asked my chief culture officer to give me an objective assessment of our gender pay equity as well as ethnic and gender diversity for our 150 employees. I was pleased to learn that we have a relatively balanced organization. We have a 65 percent female to male ratio and on a pay equity basis, our female team members are slightly better compensated on both base and total compensation than their male counterparts. We are examining opportunities to continue broadening our ethnic diversities to better represent our national market, and we would like to see continued growth in female and ethnic representation in our senior positions. I also believe that we need more formality for sensitivity training regarding sexual harassment, discrimination, mentoring and gender/ethnic inclusion. "But the journey of a thousand miles begins with a good objective assessment where opportunities can be identified.

"Fourth, resolve to change with very specific activities for yourself and your organization. "This one is the toughest. We all are creatures of habit and we have to want to be better and to do better. For my part, I have resolved to make sure that at all levels of the organization do these things: We need more awareness at all levels of the need to broaden applicant pools to include gender and ethnic diversity. And where there is an imbalance, the tie should go in the direction of creating necessary diversity.

"In other areas of potential discrimination, including those protected by law, managers at all levels need to hear from the CEO that the company's culture has a zero tolerance for discrimination of any kind, and the CEO has to lead by example. And, all managers need to be encouraged by the CEO to mentor in an inclusive way, and open dialogue with team members can help with this.

"All leaders, both men and women, need to be better listeners, especially on this topic of understanding where women face barriers to communication and advancement.

"Fifth, rid your organization of discrimination of any kind and foster inclusion at all levels.

"Our next step at CUSG and MCUL is to review department by department to see if, in some cases, we might have swung too far in one direction. If a department is almost entirely female or a certain demographic group, it might be time to diversify. Again, hiring should always be about hiring the most qualified person, but without discrimination of any kind. I also want to do a better job of creating awareness and expanding training so that all of our leaders and team members understand the 'why' behind gender and ethnic inclusion and not just the legal side to it."[102] *(Authors' note: Permission to include Adams' article in full is appreciated, and our readers are encouraged to visit him at www.cuinsight.com.)*

Career recruiter Good & Co. explores the personality strengths of male and female executives while helping companies hire the right people for the right position and empowering people to make quality career decisions. Comparing the personalities of male and female CTOs and CEOs, unveiled these insights:[103]

"We first explored a group of 358 Chief Technical Officers. Our findings suggest that male CTOs were 46 percent more grandiose and 34 percent more self-believing than women in the same role. Female CTOs were 24 percent more averse to ambiguity and 29 percent more intrinsically competitive – more likely to seek personal betterment rather than get off on competition with others. Interestingly, the opposite pattern was observed in male CTOs, who were 48 percent more motivated by outward competition. Our data suggest that female and male CTOs are equally empathic, compliant, organized, and innovative.

"Similar patterns were observed between male and female CEOs. Looking at 685 Chief Execs, we found that male CEOs were 11 percent more self-believing and 35 percent more grandiose than female CEOs. Male CEOs were also 14 percent more excitement-seeking, suggesting that, compared to women, they are more likely to be comfortable with taking risks. Female CEOs, on the other hand, were 20 percent more likely to need to feel in control of their environment – a characteristic associated with being more authoritarian. In addition to this, they were 16 percent more sympathetic compared to their male counterparts. These results are in keeping with our previous research, which found that female managers are likely to adopt a more nurturing management style coupled with maintaining a high level of authority.

"Interestingly, when we compared the female CEOs to a matched sample of non-senior female employees, the results were very much in line with Chamorro-Premuzic's findings. Female CEOs appear to be more confident, self-believing and politically minded compared to non-senior female employees. Our sample shows that, in order to climb the corporate ladder, women may assume behaviors that are traditionally associated with masculinity.[104]

In her article, "New Study Finds Men Want to Help Women at Work, But Just Don't Know How," Georgene Huang, CEO of the largest community network for women, points out, "New research from Fairygodboss surveyed 400 men and found that the majority of respondents (88 percent) say they want to help women advance in the workplace, but they don't know the best actions to take. Engaging male allies in discussions about gender diversity and equality is crucial to them understanding how to support women and feeling the drive to do so: 'Research from BCG shows that when men are deliberately engaged in gender inclusion programs, 96 percent of organizations see progress – compared to only 30 percent of organizations where men are not engaged.' When women's Employee Resource Groups (ERGs) engage male allies, they utilize positive peer pressure to spread a culture of accountability and inclusivity throughout the workplace and, ultimately, help drive towards more parity."[105]

In our research, including interviews with executive and C-suite men, we found that to attain gender balance, inclusion and parity in the workplace, men will be key drivers of the cultural shift that occur. We must challenge men to change the social and unconscious bias by choosing to promote women when they are the best, or equally qualified, candidates. How to do that? In the following chapters, we offer proprietary models and algorithms to solve this dilemma that men find themselves in.

To attain gender equity, men will play a significant role as the drivers of a cultural shift that is long overdue.

Huang continues in her article to point out key data from the recent "Women in the Workplace" report by McKinsey & Co. and LeanIn.org which states that "… unbiased hiring and promotion practices are critical to achieving gender equality. However, male respondents did not see fair hiring and promotion practices as key factors in helping women achieve equality. Male hiring managers cited 'women not applying to their jobs' and a 'lack of women in the workforce' as the top two reasons why they don't hire more women, despite the fact that women make up 47 percent of the U.S. workforce. This signals a clear disconnect between perception and reality. In fact, 39 percent of respondents say they believe the best thing they can do to help advance gender equality is to advocate for women, while only 13 percent said promoting more women and 12 percent said hiring more women. Although a nice sentiment, 'advocating for women' does not define concrete actions that men can take to help address the root causes of gender inequality. When directly asked what women can do to make it easier for men to be successful allies, half of all respondents said women should tell them what they can do to help. While this does seem to put the burden back on female employees, it also gives women the opportunity to direct company actions in a way that will best help them."[106]

Men and women working together to find the solution is the key to unlocking the cultural shift, and ultimately, realizing the transformation required for gender parity. While men are asking what they can do to help, women have the opportunity to speak up, share what works and identify the remaining C-suite obstacles that must be overcome.

SUFFRAGE 2.0:

BUILDING NEXT-CENTURY GRIT TO GET RESULTS

OBJECTIVES

The Solution: Grit

Next-century grit

Moving from Suffrage 1.0 to Suffrage 2.0

Suffrage 2.0 solutions: Individual to executive grit

Corporate grit and corporate social responsibility

CHAPTER 5:
THE SOLUTION - GRIT

Simultaneous to determining our research approach, was the ever-increasing conversation around grit and its correlation with success. You will recall the number of references to McKinsey earlier in the book regarding this complex conversation about disparities and dilemmas.

Early in Duckworth's career, she worked as a management consultant for McKinsey & Co.; however, she left to pursue a career in teaching as a seventh-grade math teacher in a New York City public school. In her 2016 bestselling book, "Grit: The Power of Passion and Perseverance," Duckworth outlines how grit is highly predictive of achievement throughout life. Her 2013 TED Talk on the subject has been watched by more than 14 million people and translated into 49 languages. During the TED Talk, Duckworth was uncertain whether grit could be built or taught. Since then, she and others, including Eskereis-Winkler (another prominent psychologist focused on goal achievement), believe that grit *can* be cultivated. What if we were to develop grit in younger women and men, even those entering the workforce; the kind of individual grit that could lead to executive grit. If grit can be cultivated, could it conceivably become a central theme in a corporation's culture, helping companies encourage grit among their employees and therefore becoming grit-driven work environments?

In editing the final copy of this book and winding down the research, co-author Christine and her husband Dave were having a conversation about the different aspects of the book. Dave expressed his sincere appreciation for the overarching theme of executive female grit and his concern with aggregating individual, executive, corporate and collective grit, instead of having a singular focus on individual grit. Christine explained the reasoning behind the larger scope, saying, "If we only captured a book about female executive grit and stories that are inspiring, it potentially ends there; another great, feel-good book that spotlights accomplished women and their road to success. By addressing the broader scope and challenging the corporate and collective entities, there's an opportunity to not only raise the roof around female executives who have made it to the C-suite, but also to challenge the collective to make real change happen. There is a significant chance that those leaders and companies with grit – executive grit – will step up and address the gaps in their organizations. When they succeed and their senior leadership teams and boards look more inclusive and diverse, other organizations can and will follow in their footsteps. It becomes a powerful movement of inclusivity."

With the number of women reaching management levels and obtaining college degrees as well as advanced certifications, why is the number of women CEOs stagnating? As mentioned earlier, only 7.4 percent of Fortune 500 companies are run by female CEOs, causing *Fortune* to launch the 100X25 initiative, which is pushing for female CEOs to lead 100 of the Fortune 500 companies by 2025. How would this be possible with the current numbers and trajectory?

Author Duckworth, a MacArthur "genius" grant winner, says, "Common sense advice is one thing, but advice that is based on rigorous scientific research is better. I created the Grit Scale so that I could study grit as a scientist because you cannot study what you cannot measure."[107] "I realize," reports *Forbes* contributor Margaret Perlis, "that the role of grit has become a 'topic du jour,' however, we seek to make it more than that … the true catalyst for change. Duckworth tweaked the definition: 'perseverance and passion for long-term goals … context of exceptional performance and success.'"[108] Co-author interviewed Angela Cody-Rouget for this book, and found the retired Air Force major and the founder of Major Mom Organizers very passionate about grit and the role it has played in her life. During the interview, Cody-Rouget emphasized that "true grit does not happen overnight." Angela's

Constitutional Grit | 105

story is compelling and one of many stories we captured that identifies the internal fortitude or grit that is required for success. Deliberate practice of all things related to grit can be found in famous words by Theodore Roosevelt, cited in "The Man in the Arena": "The credit belongs to the [wo]man who is actually in the arena, whose face is marred by dust and sweat and blood; who strived valiantly; who errs, who comes again and again, because there is no effort without error and shortcoming."[109]

Why grit

For a number of reasons, a plethora of studies have been conducted to determine the formula for achieving desired success, determining who makes it and who does not. If there was an algorithm, would it entail intellect, inherent talent, skill, IQ, EQ, and to what degree? "While none of these factors have proven to generate any kind of miracle formula, research has found evidence that over any other measurable factor, possessing the quality of grit is the highest predictor of an individual achieving greatness".[110] These are the auspices under which The Rockefeller Foundation provided a grant for Korn Ferry, a top executive search firm, to "design and execute a research project geared to developing action-oriented initiatives to create a sustainable pipeline of female CEOs."[111] A similar approach was taken, and they were able to secure the participation of 57 female CEOs, 41 from Fortune 1000 companies, and 16 from privately held organizations. The research involved collecting "pivotal experiences, either personal history and career progression, using Korn Ferry's executive online assessment to measure key personality traits and drivers that had an impact."[112]

Defining grit, characteristics of grit and individual grit

Tenacity, resolve, persistence, drive and relentless determination. Each describes grit, and most people possess it. The technical definition of grit is "a personality trait possessed by individuals who demonstrate passion and perseverance toward a goal despite being confronted by significant obstacles and distractions. Those who possess grit are able to self-regulate and postpone their need for positive reinforcement while working diligently on a task."[113]

Filled with passion and a thirst for achieving goals, women with an awareness of their own grit rise up with renewed strength and purpose, and are resolute when they've suffered failure, a setback or a time when things just didn't turn out as expected. Women with grit are passionate, persistent and filled with a sense of knowing they will find a way, even when there is, seemingly, no way. What if the path could be illuminated? What if there were a formula or algorithm that would allow women to achieve C-level positions more rapidly?

According to Duckworth, it is not innate intelligence but resolve and tenacity that create success. In other words, grit. Defined, grit is a psychological marker that identifies the possession of passion for the long game and determination to achieve an end.[149] It is the resilience to go on with renewed purpose. It is the commitment to your goals and a belief in yourself and/or to a greater cause. The beauty of grit is that it is not just a popular buzzword – it's a powerful and formidable motivational tool that can be used in both work and personal life.

Where does grit come into the picture for most women? The women we have interviewed prove that it's not feelings of worth, the overcoming of insecurities or one's title that helps them achieve the dream. It is *grit*. It is the persistence and strong-willed perseverance that has enabled women throughout history to achieve their dreams and goals. Individual grit is defined as having the courage and confidence to show the strength of your character. Executive grit, on the other hand, often means "finding perseverance and sustainable passion to work toward long-term goals, rather than growing discouraged and giving up when things do not work out as quickly as one might hope."[114] Regardless of how the term is categorized (individual or executive), we know that grit is the solution to ensuring women and men are equipped to move the needle toward inclusivity and gender parity.

Female veterans are a group that demonstrates incredible resilience with courage, optimism, creativity and most certainly confidence. Women Entrepreneurs reports that female veterans comprise 17 percent of the post-9/11 veteran population and are the fastest-growing sub-population of the veteran community, according to data from the Institute for Veterans and Military Families (IVMF). These women are also increasingly starting and growing businesses, even in the previously male-dominated STEM fields. In fact, female veterans are twice as likely to pursue STEM-related occupations as are their civilian counterparts. The research shows that high-performing entrepreneurs tend to demonstrate solid decision-making and high levels of confidence, independence and high self-efficacy, even within chaotic environments. Considering their military service background and exposure to multiple, often dangerous, environments, female veterans are well known to possess these skills. [115]

Still, female entrepreneurs encounter challenges. In an IVMF/Syracuse University study, more than 83 percent of female veterans surveyed cited obstacles in starting their own businesses. For female veterans and female professionals alike, resilience keeps women optimistic, confident and creative in situations that create challenge.

Even with more women than ever stepping into roles with higher levels of responsibility, or starting their own companies, it is still a stark reality in this leadership landscape that once a woman reaches the highest levels in a company or organization, she will likely have no other female counterparts at the same level.

Since 2012, up until very recently when she announced she would step down in 2020, IBM has had a phenomenal female CEO, Ginny Rometty, leading the charge. "Constitutional Grit" co-author Christine's career at IBM finished prior to Rometty's CEO assignment, but she was fortunate to have several female executives in her circle who were amazing trailblazers, paving the way for other women in the organization.

In 2007, after leaving an extraordinarily successful career as a transformation executive at IBM, Christine became an entrepreneur and the CEO of Brightworks Consulting. With multi-level corporate experience and a host of executive consultants under contract, Brightworks began as an executive coaching and recruiting firm, and has expanded several times over the years to accommodate industry demand and change. Today, Brightworks Consulting successfully serves the public and private sector with strategic planning, community outreach and engagement initiatives, management consulting, and a Women Leadership Institute. Christine notes, "As a female CEO, it's absolutely imperative to have resilience, optimism, courage and people who believe in you. Whether it's the CEO of a company you do business with, a potential business partner, staff working for your company or an influencer in a key industry, people want to believe in you and your mission. Do they understand what your capabilities and talents are? They are relying on you as the CEO to tell them what you can do for them. For women to succeed as CEOs, courage, optimism and resilience make the absolute difference between successfully running a company or becoming a statistic. "Recognizing the unique challenges and opportunities women face as they rise through the leadership ranks in public, private and nonprofit organizations, both domestically and on a global scale, Brightworks Consulting launched the Women in Leadership Institute in 2018. Integrating the art of leadership with professional and personal development strategies to help women at all levels of their career, WIL leverages the success of women where they are today, mixing new content focused on enhancing their business acumen with leadership skills and corporate climate astuteness. With the publishing of this book, the Brightworks institute will expand its reach to men and women running organizations who want to solve gender balance challenges in their own companies. Notes Christine, "With U.S.-based companies employing more than half of the domestic female population, we know we must do better to provide a roadmap for women and men to resolve gender equity in the C-suite."

Growing grit

Women grow grit in many ways, but two ways were significantly evident in our research. Women often grow grit from the core of who they are, through what they have experienced and by having a solid purpose. They also cultivate it by choosing a tribe of other women who have grit, and/or by surrounding themselves with both genders, those who are either grittier than or as gritty as they are.

It is no secret that who we surround ourselves with has the ability to shape our thinking, our identity and our lives. Proverbs 13:20 says, "Walk with the wise and become wise, for a companion of fools suffers harm." When we choose to be a part of a culture and engage in community that can and does overcome adversity, we develop grit and learn that even when the odds seem impossible, we can overcome.

Research has shown that neither gender bias training nor a heightened awareness of gender equality is having an effect on changing organizational behavior. By having the necessary grit to work through the differences both men and women bring to the office, and by implementing models and algorithms that will change behavior, organizations will be able to recognize the benefit of having equal representation of men and women in the C-suite.

Yes, grit is a motivational subject, often undervalued in its importance in our future and past. This chapter is intended to serve as a reminder of women's historical victories as well as the challenges that lie ahead, both of which should elevate our level of endurance and our drive toward excellence as individuals, organizations and communities. Remember, you have slayed dragons, climbed what others might consider unconquerable mountains and cracked and even broken through your own glass ceilings.

If Duckworth found grit to be the greatest predictor of success for children conquering math, then can it not also be a predictor of those who will accelerate the advancement of your organization? Executives, both male and female, make selections that often indicate a lack of understanding of the importance of creating a workforce of warriors. What happens when you put a bunch of gritty folks together? What can be accomplished?

If you are to build the best possible team, be sure to distinguish those who are gritty from those who are greedy, and those who are relentless from those who are reckless.

Making a grit assessment of yourself and others can help to drive exponential results, both personal and organizational.

CHAPTER 6:
NEXT-CENTURY GRIT

"Your past does not determine who you are. Your past prepares you for who you are to become."

Joel Osteen, pastor and author

Is it true that the best predictor of your future behavior is your past behavior? We certainly hope not. Inequality currently has severe consequences our country cannot afford to experience. Achieving equality will take significant effort, but the dividends of hard work will be worth it.

It is true the reconceptualization required to achieve success in the area of women gaining full representation and participation in the C-suite and in boardrooms across the country, not to mention around the world, will not be easy. As a matter of fact, it will be quite painful, hence the inclusion of the word "grit" in the title of this book. A possible foreshadowing of the experience ahead as these efforts are addressed in the coming years is in the conversation relative to why the "e" is missing from the word "suffrage," which more accurately conveyed what it took to achieve equal voting rights for women: suffer-age. There would be suffering and sacrificing required. Consider this historic moment, as it appears in the article, "The Women's Rights Movement, 1848–1920," which can be found in the U.S. Congress History, Art & Archives. It states: "Elizabeth Stanton drafted a 'Declaration of Sentiments, Grievances, and Resolutions' that echoed the preamble of the Declaration of Independence: 'We hold these truths to be self-evident: that all men and women are created equal.' Among the 13 resolutions set forth in Stanton's 'Declaration' was the goal of achieving the 'sacred right of franchise.'"[116]

Today, we seek to achieve full representation and participation through the sacred right of work equity. Consider the origin of the word suffrage. It is a Latin word derived from *suffragium*, meaning vote, political support and the right to vote. Suffrage 2.0 is about reconstituting the word "vote" and reimagining what it would mean for female voting to take place, not just in the political polls but also in the executive suites, organizational hallways and boardrooms around the world. What would it mean for women to vote and participate daily in critical economic and social matters that impact the country and community? How do we go about recasting and reframing our conversations and efforts toward real results such as this?

Co-author of this book Toni is blessed to work at Arizona State University, the institution she attended for undergraduate work three decades earlier. While certainly a decent institution back then, it has transformed into a more vibrant higher education experience with a real commitment to student learning, access to education and community embeddedness. As incoming university president in 2002, Michael M. Crow has led a revolution in learning that has resulted in ASU being named the country's No. 1 school for innovation six years running, as selected by leadership and educational peers from across the country and reported in *U.S. News & World Report.* We reference this because in President Crow's book, "Designing the New American University," he states that tackling large societal issues is the role of a university. A core cultural characteristic at ASU is to take on what the president calls "moonshot projects" for community and societal good.

"Captain of Moonshots" at Google X, Eric Astro Teller, is the author of "10x ss Easier than 10 percent. In it, he theorizes something that reflects the challenges faced in Suffrage 2.0: "Here is the surprising truth," he writes. "It's often easier to make something 10 times better than it is to make it 10 percent better.

"Yes… really," adds Teller. "Because when you are working to make things 10 percent better, you inevitably focus on the existing tools and assumptions. It's tempting to feel as though improving things this way means we're being good soldiers, with the grit and perseverance to continue where others may have failed, but most of the time we find ourselves stuck in the same old slog. However, when you aim for a 10x gain, you lean instead on bravery and creativity – the kind that, both literally and metaphorically, can put a man on the moon.

"Moonshot thinking starts with picking a big problem: something huge, long existing, or on a global scale. Next, it involves articulating a radical solution – one that would actually solve the problem if it existed. Finally, there needs to be some kind of concrete evidence that the proposed solution is not quite as crazy as it at first seems; something that justifies at least a close look at whether such a solution could be brought into being if enough creativity, passion, and persistence were brought to bear on it."[117]

In the process of completing the research for this book, co-author Christine was appointed to the board of directors of a national nonprofit based in Arizona. At her initial appearance as a member of the board – at a table of distinguished and successful community leaders, she noted the absence of any other females not only in attendance, but on the roster of fellow board members. Thinking back to the research underway for this book and the work she was doing in her own company, she realized that not speaking up, not taking the risk to expose the oversight could lead to the sad prospect of history repeating itself. Women have been and still are chastised for speaking up, as if they were asking for something above and beyond. So, Christine spoke up and pointed out the inequity. Taking the risk – championing greater equity on the nonprofit's board – resulted in the addition of two qualified females being added to the roster. Grit works.

Moonshot – Differentiated thinking and differentiated strategy

Both historic and current events have provided the backdrop, foundation and context for this book. There is disagreement, there is dissention – and there has always been such wrangling – when strategies necessary to effect change are discussed. The change sought represents a significant task: to successfully build gender parity in the executive-level offices of organizations across the land. Consider the following quotes and ask yourself, "How do we leverage history to accelerate our future?"

- "Women's suffrage leaders, moreover, often disagreed about the tactics and whether to prioritize federal or state reforms. Ultimately, the suffrage movement provided political training for some of the early women pioneers in Congress, but its internal divisions foreshadowed the persistent disagreements among women in Congress and among women's rights activists after the passage of the 19th Amendment."[118]

- "Just as the anniversary women's marches were preparing to set off in late January, news coverage focused on disputes about vision, goals and tactics had split the March movement, creating two separate groups: Women's March, Inc., and March On. There were promises of cooperation but whiffs of ill will between the groups."[119]

Today, we live in a society where overly politicizing important issues has stitched its way into the fabric of our everyday lives, as evidenced in headlines, reports and opinions found in local and national media, social and otherwise. As of the final editing of this book, the U.S. has experienced another record year for women's advancement in key leadership positions, as 126 women hold seats in the U.S. Congress. There is momentum building. According to a Pew Research Center survey, "Most Americans favor seeing more women in such jobs … 59 percent of adults say there are too few women in high political offices."[120] It is imperative we not be so entrenched in tradition and history and "the way it is done" that we are unable to forge our own path; to do so only contributes to the projected 200-plus year equity timeline.

> "I think society has, for centuries, trained us to think in certain ways about women and girls. It will take a long time, and it will take a persistent effort, to overcome those innate biases."
>
> *Anne Richards, CEO, M&G Investments*

One area of government is working to solve for this issue: the Executive Branch. In a recent *Forbes* article, "Hundreds of Women Have Lead Roles in the Trump administration. 45 More Await Senate Confirmation," contributor Roslyn Layton spotlights the president's Cabinet, in which women leaders include the secretaries of education, transportation, and homeland security, as well as the appointment of the first woman to head the CIA. More than 300 women were in politically appointed roles, and dozens were serving as federal judges and international ambassadors in 2019. As the business of the federal government happens across many agencies, offices and departments, there are many more instances where women are at the helm or second in command. Layton lauds the list of women in approximately 300 politically appointed roles in 2019.[122]

History has taught us the importance of creating common standards in our different approaches when constructing an aligned set of strategic design principles. While many have attempted numerous techniques and methodologies to achieve equity, diversity and parity in key organizational positions, transformation eludes us. This leads us to an inquiry as to why this type of transformation has been so elusive. Some have solved for it, others have not. Inquiry provides a different perspective.

Question of inquiry No. 1:

Could there be an opportunity to collaborate, consolidate, and coordinate rather than continue our scattered, siloed and segregated efforts? This could answer the question as to why there is such stagnation in the advancement of women to the C-suite and board appointments. What will it take for change to occur? Well, our current circumstance aligns with The World Economic Forum's projection that "it will take [another] 200 years to achieve workplace gender equality." [123]

Consider the austerity of this prediction and even this revelation that came as we were writing the book. At our current rate of change, our children and their children will not see the equality we all desire. If you have daughters or granddaughters, they will neither see nor experience this equality.

As shared in previous chapters, Suffrage 1.0 was initiated out of a call for equality relative to women's right to vote, the beginning of social and political equivalence for women, opening doors for women in industries, and participation at corporate and social levels that had not yet been experienced. Suffrage 2.0 is about moving from access and equality to full representation and participation in the world of work for qualified women.

George Friedman, founder of STRATFOR, the preeminent private intelligence and forecasting firm, wrote the book "The Next 100 Years: A Forecast for the 21st Century." In it, he lays out geopolitical predictions for the next 100 years. New world powers, wars and tensions that create new alliances are postulated for the purpose of painting a picture of what is to come. Historical social trends are proposed to have catastrophic economic impacts. But, not to worry; U.S. recovery is also predicted.

Just as technological advancements and geopolitical incidents are critical to the future of our world, so are social structures that empower and maximize human potential for half of the human race. While we will not attempt to predict the next 100 years, our goal is to set a common vision of the power and impact of fully leveraging half of the world's human capital. What prevents us from doing just that? We must understand:

1. What trends will affect women's progress toward workforce empowerment and optimization.
2. What the next 100 years look like for women in the workforce.
3. The projected representation levels of leadership for women.
4. The necessary preparation for participation and representation at the highest levels of the workforce.
5. The worst and best practices.
6. Women's potential economic contribution to society.
7. How higher representation/participation fuels the economy and spirit of a country.

Important future trends and the trajectory of women

 The projected skill gap, if not addressed, will create greater disparities and broaden the fissure in the path toward female leadership. This is because of the pipeline and preparation issues that will arise. Individual and corporate commitment is required to alter the trajectory of women as "automation, artificial intelligence, the gig economy and demographic and social shifts are changing the very nature of work, increasing their vulnerability to pay equity and leadership access in this time of rapid change."124 How can business build a "future of work" that works for women? The following projections give context to the potential impact.

- "The Future of Women at Work: Transitions in the Age of Automation," a McKinsey Co. study, suggests "Women account for more than 70 percent of workers in healthcare and social assistance, but less than 25 percent of machine operators and craft workers."[125]

- As we acclaim our continued technological prowess, "40 million-160 million women (7-24 percent) and 60 million-275 million men (8-28 percent) will need to transition to different occupations by 2030. Unsuccessfully converting/increasing necessary skills could decrease employment, worsening gender inequality."[126]

- Women hold just 19 percent of software development jobs and 21 percent of computer programmer jobs. With an obvious connection to the future of artificial intelligence and all other technological advancement efforts, increasing graduations in this high-tech programming field are essential.[127]

The opportunity and leadership gaps

There must be a formulation of intersectional, correlative and reconceptualized practices to adequately address discrimination and the lack of access for women across age, race, ethnicity, sexual orientation and other factors. Successfully implementing these structures can have tremendous impact, ensuring that women of all backgrounds are valued and supported to fully participate in and lead the workplaces of the future. Consider some of the factors emphasized by Women Deliver, a leading global advocate that champions gender equality and the health and rights of girls and women.

- Companies with greater diversity in management earned 38 percent more of their revenues, on average, over the previous three years than companies with less diversity.
- Employers who embrace diversity at all levels are more appealing to about 60 percent to 70 percent of job seekers. The job matching site CareerLabs found that job seekers increasingly value diversity and inclusion, especially at the C-suite level.
- Gender-diverse companies outperform their competitors by 21 percent.
- If 600 million more women had access to the internet, annual GDP could increase by $18 billion across 144 developing countries.
- In 2016, the Hay Group division of Korn Ferry collected data from 55,000 professionals across 90 countries and found that "women more effectively employ the emotional and social competencies correlated with effective

leadership and management than men."[28] This suggests that women may be at an advantage to compete for roles with a higher demand for so-called soft skills.

- Women represent only 25 percent of the technology workforce, and it is rare to find women in technology leadership roles.[21] Women have been excluded due to structural biases in hiring and promotions, unfair compensation and harassment, and a lack of technical skills.

- Diverse leadership is associated with better financial performance and greater innovation. According to a survey of employees at more than 1,700 companies across eight countries, companies that reported above-average diversity on their management teams also reported innovation revenue (incremental revenue due to new business) that was 19 percent higher than that of companies with below-average leadership diversity — 45 percent of total revenue versus just 26 percent.[128]

The numbers prove this. Launched recently, the "Better Leadership, Better World: Women Leading for the Global Goals" report by the Business and Sustainable Development Commission highlights the value that gender balance brings to business and our world.

As the report indicates, according to the McKinsey Global Institute, USD $28 trillion could be added to global annual GDP by 2025 if women and men were to participate equally in the economy.[129]

CHAPTER 7:

SUFFRAGE 1.0 TO SUFFRAGE 2.0

The equity timeline is estimated to be 200-plus years – twice the time that has passed since our last suffrage movement. To minimally achieve a similar level of gains realized over the past 100 years, we must put forth twice the effort, effectively doubling down on key actions toward success. Widely published *New Yorker* contributor Cep says, "The struggle for women's suffrage does not just extend further into the past than we thought; it also extends to the present, and the future. The uncertainty of the suffrage victory foreshadows the precariousness of voting rights today, when even those who supposedly have the right are often prevented from exercising it. Disenfranchisement can take many forms, and its most insidious manifestations are regrettably common: purging voter rolls, passing voter-identification requirements, understaffing or closing polling places, gerrymandering voting districts. Under the circumstances, perhaps the best way to celebrate the anniversary of the passage of the Nineteenth Amendment is to remember all those who cannot vote, not only those who can."[166] This book is about extending that right to those who have not had equitable opportunity. After more than 25 years of exemplary work experience, training male counterparts, attaining multiple advanced educational degrees, women are still not positioned to vote outside of the political polls. They are successfully achieving double-digit revenue growth, building teams that are performing at maximum capacity, but still have limited C-suite opportunity. How do we accelerate toward a faster path for equal participation and representation?

Question of inquiry No. 2:

So, how do we deploy a 2.0 scalable operation? This quote from "How Business Can Build a Future of Work that Works for Women" encapsulates how a person, organization, country and community might transition from Suffrage 1.0 to Suffrage 2.0:

"Given the urgency and complexity of the challenges ahead, we need collective action that starts today. While greater evidence will help us to understand the potential effects of these shifts, it is certain the changing world of work will influence employees, employers, markets, local and national economies, and communities. It is also certain that work-related disruptions will have unique implications for women. With business, government and civil society intentionally building gender-aware strategies, there is an opportunity to overcome existing systemic constraints to women's economic empowerment. By starting today and working together, we can shape a future of work that works for women."[130]

Grit as the catalyst for ensuring full representation and participation in C-suites and boardrooms expands and deepens the original grit model, fueling the next generation of awareness, executive grit and investment action.

> Executive Grit + Corporate Grit + Collective Grit = Suffrage 2.0: Next Generation Grit Practices for Full Participation and Representation

Next-generation grit: Practices for full participation and representation

The gains made during the Suffrage 1.0 movement were greatly the result of individual grit and the sacrifices made to lift up other women. To ensure Suffrage 2.0 is on a positive trajectory, organizations must take the lead by focusing on the building up of systems and people for the meaningful advancement of women's full participation and representation in executive-level positions. Consider the recent events and conversations held by the Business Roundtable, a group of prominent CEOs from top U.S. companies. Jamie Dimon, chairman and CEO of JPMorgan Chase and chairman of the Business Roundtable, is widely respected for his innovation, business acumen and social impact. Dimon made the following observation at this event:

> **The American dream is alive, but fraying, major employers are investing in their workers and communities because they know it is the only way to be successful over the long term. These modernized principles reflect the business community's unwavering commitment to continue to push for an economy that serves all Americans."[131]**

Two hundred U.S. CEOs representing some of the nation's largest companies, including Amazon, American Airlines, JPMorgan Chase, and Johnson & Johnson, recently issued a joint "Statement on the Purpose of a Corporation." The statement represents a commitment by these executive leaders to lead their companies for the benefit of all stakeholders: customers, employees, suppliers, communities and shareholders. A brief excerpt from the statement:

> "Americans deserve an economy that allows each person to succeed through hard work and creativity and to lead a life of meaning and dignity. We believe the free-market system is the best means of generating

good jobs, a strong and sustainable economy, innovation, a healthy environment and economic opportunity for all … We commit to deliver value to all of them, for the future success of our companies, our communities and our country.[132]

This preamble was followed by four bullets detailing the primary principles, the second of which states, "Investing in our employees. This starts with compensating them fairly and providing important benefits. It also includes supporting them through training and education that help develop new skills for a rapidly changing world. We foster diversity and inclusion, dignity and respect".[133] Following the adoption of the new creed, Johnson & Johnson's CEO, Alex Gorsky, stated, "It affirms the essential role corporations can play in improving our society when CEOs are truly committed to meeting the needs of all stakeholders."[134]

It is now commonplace to find statements of corporate social responsibility on the websites of many organizations, both for-profit and nonprofit. This deeper and public-facing commitment to taking accountability for the improvement of our society must also encourage transformation through a meaningful investment in diversity and inclusion as outlined in the different statements of purpose, mission statements and value propositions posted by local, national and international businesses. This recognition of accountability to workforce and community means our grit must be taken to a new level in order to nurture and produce the next generation of workplace leadership.

McKinsey's 10-year longitudinal study, "Women Matter – Time to Accelerate," notes: "Despite a strong case for gender parity, both at the macroeconomic level and for business performance, the level of gender inequality is high, and sometimes extremely high around the world."[136] Representation of women on corporate boards and executive committees, as of 2017, indicates that the U.S. ranks eighth among G20 countries. Considering our stature and standing as the most powerful country on earth, does this ranking represent our collective capabilities, critical leadership and an optimization of our country's human assets?

U.S. News and World Report, in partnership with BAV Group and the Wharton School of the University of Pennsylvania, has created metrics to rank the world's most powerful countries in its annual "Best Countries" rankings. The measuring stick includes five key attributes: military alliances, international alliances, political influence, economic influence, and leadership. Conversely, another report, "The World in 2050: Quantifying the Shift in the Global Economy" predicted a seismic shift in the rankings, anticipating the U.S. will drop to the No. 2 position. Using macroeconomist Robert Barro's research, GDP projections included in the report are modeled using "key determinants" such as economic governance, income per capita, human capital and starting level of income per capita. Accordingly, the U.S. is projected to be the second richest economy in the world in 2050, with a GDP of $22.27 trillion and a per capita income of $55,134. The projected growth per capita income for the U.S. is lower than other developed economies because its-already rich infrastructure "constrains growth." For so long the richest country on the planet, the U.S. will have to contend with being "second best."[137]

In the previous paragraph, leadership was mentioned as the fifth key element to the *U.S. News & World Report* country rankings. Although no formal correlation was made between leadership and the Year 2050 world ranking research, it certainly stands out as we consider GDP and per capita income. "The case for gender parity in the economy and in the workplace has never been so strong," reads the "World in 2050" report. "We need to remove those persistent barriers which exist in and outside the workplace. And we need to build the conditions and mind-sets in our societies."[138]

The current mindset drastically undervalues how women's rights not only contribute to economic development but actually drive it. Women's participation in economic growth "is treated as a happy consequence of development; something that should be fostered and encouraged, but not necessary for a country's success."[139]

Women are a huge untapped source of economic growth. Unlocking their full potential will require concerted action by both public and private sectors. There is a huge range of actions that can catalyze the economic potential of women. Recognition that leaving the economic status quo unchallenged and unchanged is not an option.

Council on Foreign Relations, "Empowering Women will Drive Economic Growth," May 2016[140]

The next suffrage century requires catalyzation of concerted action, challenging all we know and necessitating a new level of grit by every organization and every leader. Suffrage 2.0 requires what we call "Corporate Social Responsibility x 2 = Corporate Social Responsibility 2.0."

CHAPTER 8:

SUFFRAGE SOLUTIONS 2.0 – FROM INDIVIDUAL TO EXECUTIVE GRIT

A determining characteristic of those who enter the C-suite is something known as an executive presence, which we shared earlier in this book. For those who have experienced or witnessed it, it is a confidence and a certain savvy that comes from the responsibility and accountability of the role. Could the key ingredient to holding an executive position be executive presence, coupled with executive grit? Do both men and women possess these traits of executive presence and grit? Would they be applying for an open C-suite or board position based on qualifications? Not necessarily.

The Working Mother Research Institute recently found that "many women are less likely to have a clear sense of how to get ahead compared to their male colleagues. They lack access to information about career trajectories that would pave their way to the executive suite and aren't as aware of available career-advancement and mentorship programs."[141] The institute's study also reports, "Majorities of women who'd never held a P&L job cited a male-dominated culture (64 percent) and gender bias (54 percent) as obstacles to their advancement. The most cited barriers included lack of training, lack of understanding about the career path, and lack of information about open jobs."[142]

There are work and social skills that work to advance a woman into an executive-level leadership position. However, top leadership requires executive grit, which most women possess, whether they identify with it or not. To date, there has not been a formalized definition of executive grit, but, drawing from an article published by *Inc.*, the authors have created one. In the article, "5 Essential Traits of Leaders with True Grit," author, Bill Murphy Jr. hypothesizes that "passion and tenacity are in fact valuable traits in the notion of grit. But how do you know if you're gritty or just bull-headed?" Referencing a *Wall Street Journal* article, Mitchell adds, "Experts recommend that overly gritty types seek frank feedback about their behavior from internal mentors, business acquaintances or knowledgeable relatives."[143]

The *WSJ* article suggests conducting a self-assessment to determine the effectiveness or precision with which one applies grit. Grit alone does not ensure executive-level achievement; however, executive grit significantly increases the odds of achieving that status. How would a male or female on the C-suite trajectory know whether they possess true executive grit or are, instead, being "difficult"? Writer Murphy suggests speaking with colleagues and asking very direct questions to assess whether one's personal passion or self-interest is outpacing the good of the group.

While further considering executive grit, we returned to the writings and hypotheses of Angela Duckworth. Duckworth developed something she called the grit scale. We have taken it one step more, aligning grit (according to Duckworth) and executive grit (from our perspective).

"You gain strength, courage and confidence by every experience in which you really stop to look fear in the face. You are able to say to yourself, 'I have lived through this horror. I can take the next thing that comes along.' You must do the thing you think you cannot do."

Eleanor Roosevelt, political figure, diplomat, activist

EXECUTIVE GRIT MODEL

ANGELA DUCKWORTH
GRIT SCALE

New ideas and projects sometimes **distract** me from previous ones.

Setbacks don't discourage me. **I don't give up** easily.

Setbacks don't discourage me. I don't give up easily.

I often set a goal but later choose to pursue a different one.

I am a hard worker

I have difficulty **maintaining my focus** on projects that take more **than a few months** to complete.

My interests change from year to year.

I am diligent. I never give up.

I have been obsessed with a certain idea or project for a short time but later lost interest.

EXECUTIVE
GRIT MODEL

Executive focus and single mindedness
- Cognitive Control
- Personalized employee engagement

Executive failure and reflective practice
- Failure resume
- Reflection – a conscious form of practice

Executive approach to goal setting
- Symphonic goal setting
- Cross-disciplinary planning and operations

How executives work
- Executive productivity – time management and operational pulse points
- Executive leaders measure their success

Executive Functioning
4 core behaviors – decision making, impactful engagement, proactivity, reliability

Do CEOs obsess, and if so, how is it manifested? Obsessions become opportunities.

The Female Factor – Assessment an the organizational leadership landscape

Executive Grit Model ©

Executive focus/single-mindedness

In a 2013 *Harvard Business Review* article, "The Focused Leader," emotional intelligence expert Daniel Goleman does an outstanding job defining focus, aligning executive actions to those definitions with the scientific support around brain functions. "When we speak about being focused, we commonly mean thinking about one thing while filtering out distractions"[144] which is demonstrated above in the executive grit scale. Drawing on neuroscience research, Goleman notes, "Humans focus in many ways, drawing on different neural pathways which can be categorized into three broad areas – focusing on yourself/self-control, focusing on others, and focusing on the wider world – all of which are essential leadership skills."[145] The Rutgers University professor elaborates further on the area of cognitive control. A solution in itself, "Cognitive control is the scientific term for putting one's attention where one wants it and keeping it there in the face of temptation to wander. This focus is one aspect of the brain's executive function, which is located in the prefrontal cortex. A colloquial term for it is 'will power.' Good cognitive control can be seen in people who stay calm in a crisis, tame their own agitation, and recover from a debacle or defeat."[146]

Also consistent with single-mindedness is the ability to engage people how and when they need to be engaged. You have seen it in dynamic leaders who are natural engagers. Whether the exchange is with the custodian or the board chair, these leaders consistently exhibit actions grounded in cognitive empathy, emotional empathy and empathic concern. "Effective mentoring, managing clients, reading group dynamics, explaining themselves in a meaningful way – executives who can effectively focus on others emerge as natural leaders regardless of organizational or social rank."[147]

Executive failure

> **"The heaviness of being successful was replaced by the lightness of being a beginner again, less sure about everything. It freed me to enter one of the most creative periods of my life."**
>
> *Steve Jobs, co-founder, Apple*

Perfection is not possible in any industry, career or relationship. Failure can happen, and when it does, executives respond in unique and different ways. This is part of the solution when moving from Suffrage 1.0 to 2.0. "The experience of failure can be transformative in ways that success is not,"[148] says Jean Case, author of "Most every successful person has a story of excruciating failure in their past – and for good reason." Adds the executive businesswoman and chairman of the board of directors of *National Geographic*, "If you examine the life of anyone who has achieved something extraordinary, chances are you'll find a story of failure somewhere along the way."[149]

Essential to executive grit is a "failure resume." As with all résumés, there is chronological detail, but this résumé is a mental background of your struggles, mistakes, missteps and missed goals. The key is not the ability to simply recall your failures – or to wallow in the failures – but to constructively reflect on each as a learning exercise, a chance to consider what went wrong and how to remedy the gaffe in the future.. Think: Were there trends in behaviors, actions or thinking, and were any of these corrected from one experience to the next?

Did Steve Jobs, co-founder of Apple and innovator extraordinaire, have a failure résumé? Perhaps one of the most public failures was his dismissal from Apple. His response was, "The heaviness of being successful was replaced by the lightness of being a beginner again, less sure about everything. It freed me to enter one of the most creative periods of my life."

What if failure is the key to success? Any number of new executives fail because they "misread and misjudge the dynamics, expectations, and requirements of their new company and new role, and as a consequence missteps, mismatched expectations and cultural mis-estimation lead to an erosion of the early support base and increased polarization. Often, the organization overtly or subliminally conspires to derail the new incumbent."

A Korn Ferry Institute study of the top 1,000 U.S. companies, based on revenues, was conducted in late 2016. It examined the age and tenure of individuals holding C-suite titles and was further broken down by industry – consumer, energy, financial services, industrial, life sciences, professional services and technology. When analyzed in aggregate, the average age for a C-suite executive was 54, and the average tenure 5.3 years. Failure cannot be completely eliminated, however the way one recovers from failure and mitigates its impacts are derivatives of one's ability to retain the lessons learned from each of those failures. Learning from failures is not a new concept, however the consistency with which one documents and reflects this learning is critical.

Reflective learning is not new. John Dewey (1933), an educational pioneer, honed this concept primarily for teachers to advance and accelerate their ability to teach, which is consequential to student learning. He maintained, "We do not learn from experience. We learn from reflecting on experience."[150] Dewey asked educators to stand back from routine and move into a more conscious form of practice. Executive grit requires this heightened consciousness and discipline in developing more effective daily practices. You, too, can accelerate your own teaching and your own learning through journaling. A handbook for the exercise can be found in contributor Mary Morrissey's 2016 *Huffington Post* article, "The Power of Writing Down Your Goals and Dreams." In the piece, Morrissey highlights a study conducted by a Dominican University psychology professor who found that "you become 42 percent more likely to achieve your goals and dreams simply by writing them down on a regular basis."[151]

Executive goal setting

While executive goal setting seems to be an obvious part of any professional career plan, how many executives and up-and-coming leaders practice the important exercise with rigor and grit? The internet abounds with papers written and experts espousing the importance of effective goal setting, how to set executive goals and why goal setting is critical to a project's success.

What about goal setting for executive grit? There are acronyms like "SMART" goals – Specific, Measurable, Achievable, Realistic, Timely – and there are even project management digital resources like "smartsheet" software, but nothing is smart about setting goals in a silo or monolithic fashion. *Deloitte Insights,* a publication featuring thought leadership insight from the financial consulting giant, recently posted "The Symphonic C Suite: Teams Leading Teams." In the piece, contributor Jamal Abforouch writes, "Senior leaders must get out of their silos and work with each other more. To navigate today's constantly changing business environment and address cross- disciplinary challenges, the company's top leaders must act as one. We call this new, collaborative, team-based senior executive model the 'symphonic C Suite.'"[152]

Changing technology, broadening global markets, consumer scrutiny and expectations have created an environment where competition is at an all-time high. "If an executive team does not operate as an integrated decision-making unit with goals across lines of business that line up, they risk moving too slowly to align the organization with the demands of its time and place." This integrated approach requires executive grit and can be an effective tool for long-term planning as well, as demonstrated by Cummins Power Systems, where the C-suite worked tightly to build a 15-year plan with specific gritty goals for its products, services and business model, helping it to maintain its market leadership and renowned employment brand for many decades.

Returning to *Deloitte Insights*' "The Symphonic C Suite," results from the company's two-year global research on human capital trends were introduced. One of the findings: C-suite collaboration and goal alignment were identified as the most important issue; 51 percent of respondents rated it as very important. "Additionally, we found that respondents at organizations with the highest level of CXO cross-collaboration and aligned goals were the most likely to anticipate growth of 10 percent or more," Noted author Abforoush. While his report did not specifically reference gender equity or C-suite inequalities, it identifies a best practice for executive grit success: collaborative alignment as a necessary tool of success. Such alignment and collaboration requires leaders at all levels in the organization, both male and female, to work together for the betterment of the company. And yet 73 percent of the respondents of the Deloitte study reported that their C-suite leaders "rarely, if ever, work together on projects or strategic initiatives."[153]

Executive productivity and time management

"Where and how CEOs are involved determines what gets done. It signals priorities," say authors Nitin Noriah and Michael Porter of a *Harvard Business Review* entry under the headline "How CEOs Manage Time." "Chief executives have tremendous resources at their disposal, but they face an acute scarcity in one critical area: Time."[154] Yes, the grit scale relates to hard work, which we would agree is essential to success, but it does not always result in success. So, it is not only about working hard, it is about working smart – this is the discipline of doing.

What exactly does that mean when striving toward the C-suite? Found in the *HBR* article are answers to long-held questions about how CEOs spend their time, and their effective use of time to accommodate work-life balance, helping to ensure their work remains meaningful. This 12-year study[155] revealed findings we believe are relevant to our executive grit model. These findings are not gender specific, yet they play a key role in finding the solutions to achieving gender parity, using grit as a catalyst. The findings, sourced directly from the *HBR* study, include the following:

1. Running a global company is an exceedingly complex job. The job is consuming. The average number of hours worked daily is 9.7, with an additional 4 hours per day on the weekends, for a total of 62.5 hours per week.

2. It is vital for CEOs to block off meaningful amounts of uninterrupted time alone.

3. CEOs slept an average of 6.9 hours per day and many had regular exercise regimens.

4. Agenda driven: A clear and effective agenda optimizes the CEO's limited time. The study found that CEOs invested significant time on activities that furthered their agendas – 43 percent on average, a range from 14 percent to 80 percent time investments. CEOs expressed that the more

time they spent on their agendas, the better they felt about their use of time.

People Matters, an international thought leader in the arena of people and the workplace, states simply, "In the lexicon of management, the CEO is the epitome of leadership."[216] That being said, it would make sense that if a CEO or similar C-suite leader were to place a priority on gender parity in the workplace, then steps would be taken by those responsible to ensure the vision, the directive, the priority is addressed and realized. Is gender parity a priority? Is equal pay across genders a priority? Is promoting women to leadership and C-suite positions a priority?

Executive grit involves the management of one's own time and the ability to project that onto others. A simple example: The discipline involved in carving out valuable time to meet with direct reports was something co-author Toni learned from the chief academic officer and provost at Grand Canyon University in Phoenix. When overseeing large operational areas, these one-on-one conversations were vital operational meetings during which goals, objectives and progress – among other management issues – were discussed and updated: the determination of various projects' status, and what actions were necessary to the successful completion of each; reviews of key departmental/division performance indicators and any necessary actions required to maintain alignment with those indicators; and assessments of leader progression. These discussions were the CAOs way of providing consistent feedback, presenting and driving the agenda and its priorities, but most importantly taking time to support the workplace team. What made these so effective were the consistency with which they were held (they were rarely canceled) and the fact that preparing for these meetings constituted a personal assessment of one's own performance.

In Toni's transition to Arizona State University, similarly, the senior vice president of ASU Educational Outreach and Student Services, responsible for a voluminous portfolio that included hundreds of millions of dollars in facility assets and hundreds of millions in operational budget, provided a regular platform for executive-level team members to experience and benefit from one-on-one work discussions. However, he extended his time and attention not only through meetings with direct reports but also *their* direct reports, those responsible for significant initiatives and large operational portfolios. Co-author Toni, as deputy vice president of EOSS, prepares for these meetings with a 1:1 agenda, printouts of concise updates, allowing for a great deal of operational real estate to be covered within 30 minutes to an hour. Effective executives hold team members accountable for efficient use of this time, as it is not a time to "chit chat" but to understand the state of the operational unit. When done efficiently and consistently, these discussions can become an extremely effective leadership tool. These are not new concepts, and effective executives are consistent with this practice.

Executive measures and productivity – Finish what you start

Part of pushing a movement forward from Suffrage 1.0 to 2.0 is the ability to execute a strategy. Executive grit requires a commitment to execute with grit and shrewdness and practical knowledge, the ability to make good judgments, produce results and measure the outcomes. In an age when the sheer volume of emails and other internal-network messaging tools, phone calls, texts messages, meetings and "fire-drill" disasters, a perpetual feeling of "behindedness," can occur, says Sujan Patel. In a survey conducted with over 250 executives of industry-leading companies such as Adobe, American Express, FedEx, and HP, each emphasized having a certain "routine" designed to maximize their own productivity. Each executive mentioned exercise as essential, and Virgin Group CEO Sir Richard Branson believes it has the ability to extend or enhance your productive time by up to four hours in some cases. Seventy percent of questioned CEOs were said to eat breakfast, and all leveraged their commute to the office to be productive.

Interesting is the use of the first few hours in the office. The article "Daily Routines of Fortune 500 Leaders" reports that the majority of those surveyed dedicate about 25 minutes of their morning to strategizing and planning for the day, week, month or year. Many will document their day's hits and misses to help get things out of their heads and allow for each to be revisited in a more productive manner. "Before leaving the office each night, Ken Chenault, CEO of American Express, takes time to reflect and write down three things that he wants to accomplish the next day."[156] Successful leaders are not random in how they approach their day. They are intentional in their physical and psychological regimens that boost and optimize productivity. It is not creating a routine, it is having a ritual – an established or prescribed procedure, a series of actions performed in a fixed order. This seems simple, but we all know it takes grit to have the discipline to do this. Moving from where we are today in gender equity issues to a better place of equality in the executive workplace will require this same kind of grit.

Certainly, success means different things to different people. There is no shortage of articles sharing perspectives of executives' personal measures of success – happiness, family, reaching or surpassing their own goals and ambitions. Through the lens of executive grit, it is helpful to more clearly define business measures of success. *Inc.'s* 2018 article features the "5 Performance Indicators Every CEO Should Be Tracking":[157]

1. Net profits
2. Revenue and revenue growth rates
3. Employee engagement
4. Net promoter score - an index that measures the willingness of customers to recommend a company's products or services to others
5. Order of project fulfillment

Executive functioning

This may be considered one of the most important aspects of the C-suite agency. Although executive functioning is already a well-established concept, let's first begin with its technical definition: a set of processes that all have to do with managing oneself and one's resources in order to achieve a goal; neurologically based skills involving mental control and self-regulation. In the *Harvard Business Review* article "What Sets Successful CEOs Apart," Dina Wang, one of the authors, warns, "The behaviors we're about to describe sound deceptively simple. But the key is to practice them with maniacal consistency, which our work reveals is a great challenge for many leaders."[158] Why would they say this? The corporate leadership landscape at the turn of the century (2000-2013) was highlighted by forced turnover within the CEO position. Shareholders are said to have lost an estimated $112 billion dollars from among the world's largest 2,500 companies. The four functions the authors outline are critical to the individual aspirations of those pursuing top level positions (male or female), but also have an economic impact resulting in the greater scrutiny of a CEO's performance:

1. Making decisions with speed and conviction. "Good CEOs realize that a wrong decision may be better than no decision at all. There is no perfect answer, just perfect decisiveness." Impact: Mistakes as a result of a bad decision are somewhat expected, but not commonly a fireable offense. "We found that among CEOs who were fired over issues related to decision-making, only one-third lost their jobs because they'd made bad calls; the rest were ousted for being indecisive."

2. Engaging for impact. Do not merely engage people, engage for impact. "… CEOs who deftly engaged stakeholders in a results-oriented manner were 75 percent more successful in the role."[223] Stakeholders are both internal and external, above and below you in an organization. When executives engage, they do so with the intent of creating a value proposition toward a symphonic mindset and pursuit of organizational goals. Successful CEOs have been known

to create what are called stakeholder maps, planning and strategizing around each interaction.

3. Adapting proactively. Executives who are able to respond to increased market demands, shifting political environments and changing technology are 6.7 times more likely to succeed.[224] Adaptability is not a newly identified core skill for executives. It has, however, become even more critical, and even a differentiator, given the competitive landscape of innovation. Adaptability is grit. Stated more succinctly, "As a CEO you are constantly faced with situations where a playbook simply cannot exist. You'd better be ready to adapt," says Dominic Barton, global managing partner of McKinsey & Co. Executive grit requires that a C-suite member, or one seeking to acquire that position, will spend least 50 percent of their time thinking about the long term, based on a broad network of information.

4. Delivering reliably. Getting consistent, predictable results is said to be the most important of the four executive functions. The grit comes in the executive actions required to get there, building the right structures and recruiting the right human assets. Paramount are systems such as productive meetings, dashboards of metrics, clear accountability and other channels for monitoring performance and making rapid course corrections."

Executive obsession

"Transforming today's challenges into tomorrow's opportunity" is noted in the *HBR* article "Four Concerns That Keep CEO's Awake at Night." Challenges come in the form of complexities with globalization, talent shortages, the future of work and the pressure created through political positioning. With the heightened scrutiny around organizational transparency, even slight ethical missteps can erode the public's/consumer's trust in a matter of seconds, as social media now exponentially increases an audience's exposure to the mistake at hand. Today's challenges can come in the form of gender inequity in an organization. Cultural openness, awareness and responsiveness are critical. Employees are recognizing the disparities and raising concerns, yet executives without the experience to resolve such a dilemma may lack the tools to address fundamental inequalities within their organization. Tapping into the best practices outlined in this book can eliminate a potential misstep before it occurs.

The female factor /the CEO pipeline project by Korn Ferry

Part of the momentum in the social movement taking place across the nation today comes from organizations like the National Association for Female Executives and others that are assessing the environments of key organizations to better understand the disparity. Korn Ferry is one such organization. The key findings of "Women CEOs Speak," a new report from the Korn Ferry Institute, points also to the importance of sponsors and mentors in preparing women for leadership positions. Conducted from February to July in 2017, Korn Ferry sought to identify what qualities drive those women who comprise the current 5 percent of U.S. CEOs. The study included extensive interviews with 38 current and 19 former CEOs. The participants are or were at Fortune 500 companies (23), Fortune 1000 companies (18) and privately held companies (16). Two-thirds of the study participants also had psychometric assessments.[159]

There is a certain level of packaging and visibility [involved]" to rise to CEO," states Jane Edison Stevenson, co-author of the report. "It's not just what you know or who you know, but who knows what you know,"[160] and women need to be comfortable networking, talking about their accomplishments, and expressing their interest in taking on greater roles at their organizations. This becomes a key element to the movement. Emily Snell, president of identity protection leader InfoArmor, agrees, saying, "Women have to be their own champion. Seek out male and female mentors in your industry and organization. Opportunities will be presented, seize them!"[161] Yet, despite the record numbers of women graduating from college and entering the workforce who may be seizing these opportunities, the data still points to a "leaky pipeline," a large chasm between the women who start out on the professional track and those who ultimately advance to senior positions. And the small percentage of women who do make it to CEO benefited from holding other leadership roles first, what Stevenson calls "critical-passage" roles: "When you are marketing something in the world, you market it to the audience you're speaking to … it has not occurred to us to think how we are going to articulate [leadership] roles that connect with this audience of women leaders. There are key roles in most organizations that are viewed as critical-passage kinds of roles and there are very limited numbers of those roles … It takes a good 10 to 15 years to develop to become a CEO because you need several different types of roles to [showcase] your ability to lead the company overall."[162]

Providing women with sponsors and mentors at each of these pivotal decision points are two of the many ways that we can help to 'leak-proof' the pipeline. That is, having people in positions of influence who can actively support, sponsor and guide the career paths of women as they progress through their careers. Some interesting statistics:

- 5 percent of Fortune 1000 CEOs are female.
- 14 percent of female CEOs attribute their success to mentors.

- 12 percent of female CEOs knew they wanted to be a CEO.

Out of this data, here are additional findings. Some women were sent to executive education programs. Only two, however, described what we would consider best-in-class sponsorship with extensive opportunities for coaching and development that prepared them as CEO successors. Even when sponsorship was opaque or haphazard, it was better than no sponsorship at all. Four women mentioned an absence of sponsorship at senior levels as a hindrance to their career.

One specific example of the effects of sponsorship/mentorship comes from interviewee Angela Cody, CEO of Major Organizers, and a U.S. Air Force veteran. She shares how mentors gave her a different perspective on her life and career: "Anyone with true grit knows you do not climb up any wall by yourself. The most valuable information I gleaned from all of them could only come from someone with outside perspective. It is impossible to see what others can see because you are too close and intimate with all the details of your career, life and business. I rebranded my company twice thanks to a few mentors. First, from Organized 4 Life to Major Mom. I then went onto Major Organizers after appearing on [TV's] "Shark Tank" and listening to not only the Sharks but also Aaron Kennedy, founder of Noodles & Company; Mary, a franchisor; and a couple other women with grit."

Sponsors, too, can offer more transparency around their actions and assignments. Cross-business and cross-functional assignments, for instance, are much more effective if the women know they are being groomed for top leadership. We must note, however, that one mentor cannot provide everything. We should encourage women to seek out and invest in several such relationships, and leaders of women can make those connections for them if their network is limited.

Another interviewee, Police Chief Williams, says that "Sponsorship requires some level of commitment, but not a great deal of time. As assistant chief, I had a few notable mentors, the first of whom was a female, Commander Marsha Forient, [who was] instrumental in charting my course. A mentor invests in you, cares about you and your journey, your success. I'm currently serving as part of the venture development program in the ASU Entrepreneurs program. I'm invested in these young entrepreneurs and care about their success."

Another CEO we interviewed, Gabriel's Angels' Gaber, agrees, saying, "A mentor may also advocate for their mentee, as that is a natural byproduct of the relationship. In this instance, it is like a referral that you make because you know the person and thereby are putting your reputation on the line. It must be more than just promoting your protégé to the executive team." It is vital for women with their sights set on executive offices to have a sponsor who will support and endorse advancement.

All in agreement? Of course! A social movement takes more than sponsorship, however. Some of the women we spoke to underestimated how much personal endorsement they would need to reach the threshold of the CEO's office. Men, these women realized, not only sell themselves more aggressively, they champion one another constantly. When a man positions himself to become CEO, one woman noted, he talks about his track record — and lists 15 people who will sing his praises.

The female CEOs we interviewed were clear about the area where they felt they could have been better prepared: experience with boards and other external stakeholders. Sponsors of CEO candidates can help women get these vital experiences, thereby supporting the momentum of this vitally important social movement toward leadership.

Evelyn Orr, co-author of "Women CEOs Speak," and the vice president and chief operating officer at Korn Ferry Institute, comments further that it is "critical for women to have mentors to provide encouragement, feedback and guidance, and to have sponsors who can open career doors."[163] Late-career sponsors provide crucial shepherding at the senior executive level. Important relationships shift away from mentors who offer encouragement and advice, often outside the organization, to sponsors who take a hands-on role in managing career moves and promoting executives to the board. The CEO interviewees had much more to say about these valuable sponsors. Many women could list multiple names, most frequently including their predecessor CEO (15), other senior executives (12), board members (6) and CEOs from other companies (5). Women who had board mentors were particularly appreciative of that insight and support.

Leaders at all levels in today's organizations can take this advice and apply it immediately: Take the time to share how women are perceived by critical stakeholders and help them build the strong personal brand they need to have influence and impact. Discuss promotions and target roles in terms that appeal to the woman's ambitions and values, which likely include larger purpose, impact on people's lives, growing talent and building a positive culture.

Female factor assessment

What if you could predict whether the organization in which you work or aspire to work for has a "female factor"? Are there female influencers, and where are they located – both physically and organizationally? Indicators of influence include distribution of work or departmental assignment, operational budgets, pay and personal recognition of female leaders from the CEO/board. Assessing, understanding and navigating the leadership landscape takes surgical precision. Top of mind is the "Goldilocks Principle," which has been applied to economics and climate change, and can certainly benefit women seeking and/or maintaining their C-suite seat, also known as the "Goldilocks Zone." The principle states that something must fall within certain margins, as opposed to reaching extremes. Communication, pushing performance, raising issues and positing solutions must be done consistently in the Goldilocks Zone – not too hot, not too cold, but just right. Your tools and techniques may change daily depending upon the organizational culture and leadership landscape.

Summary

Never underestimate your personal capability in terms of leading change in any circumstance. Your voice is important. You can help people around you; this is what leaders are for. Leaders are here to empower people, to accelerate positive change, not only in themselves but also in individuals and society surrounding them.

CHAPTER 9:
CORPORATE GRIT AND CORPORATE SOCIAL RESPONSIBILITY 2.0

Change, more specifically, organizational change, was a formal discipline until the 1990s, when psychologists began to investigate the impact of economic and technical factors on people as a group and behavior as an organization. For corporations to pivot, they must be able to anticipate and address challenges even before they occur. In today's economic environment, being reactive is not sufficient; companies must be constantly seeking the competitive edge.

Let's talk competition

In her article, "How Gender Equality is a Growth Engine for the Global Economy," Renee Morad reports, "An investment in women is an investment in us all. In fact, if U.S. companies hired and promoted women at the same rate as countries like Norway, the economy can grow by 8 percent, according to S&P Global".[164] In addition, she reports on findings related to global competition:

- Around the world, gender-diverse companies are 15 percent more likely to earn more than their competitors, according to McKinsey & Co.
- Just by adding more women to the workforce, the global GDP could go up by 26 percent, according to McKinsey Global Institute.
- In India alone, women could grow the economy by up to 60 percent, according to McKinsey Global Institute.
- In the last 20 years, the revenue of women-owned U.S. companies has increased by 103 percent, according to American Express.

This leads us to our next question of inquiry.

Question of inquiry No. 3:

Can competition spur C-suite change? Can competition shift the mindsets of organizations that have not made gender diversity a formal, documented and actionable business priority?

Freelance journalist and NBC News contributor Renee Morad writes in an online piece for the network, "Despite recent advances in female board participation globally, gender diversity among top executives remains disappointingly low across all markets, with some improvement discerned in the past few years. When considering international governance, the ISS Environmental & Social Quality Score reports that 'The U.S. lags behind gender diversity policy disclosure for senior management.'"[165] Consider the fact that the S&P 500 indicates the U.S. third from the bottom, with only 32 percent of our companies having disclosed gender diversity policies for senior management. Fortune Knowledge Group conducted a survey in 2016, specifically inquiring about gender equity in Fortune 100 and 500 companies. "Nearly 70 percent of our respondents say their organization pursues an explicit women's talent strategy, with strong support across the board and high-profile efforts to create an inclusive, high-performance culture. But surprisingly, few executives indicate that their company has translated these policies into practical actions. Only about half say their firms employ transparent, gender-neutral hiring criteria, have transparent processes for identifying high potential candidates, offer maternity leave beyond legal minimums (paternity leave ranks lower still), or track gender diversity at key career milestones."[166]

As a whole, the vast majority of organizations, public or private, for profit or nonprofit, claim gender diversity is a priority, though only 79 percent have identified it as a formal business priority.[167] Those making a real commitment to full representation and participation by women have done so by going beyond mere policymaking, implementing measurable recruiting and hiring goals, making programming investments and revolutionizing the "E" factor: the environment. IBM's Institute for Business Value has identified these companies as "First Movers," because they understand the importance of the advancement of women.

Underrepresentation has moved from a moral imperative to an economic one. Only 12 percent of 2,300 companies have formal business efforts documented and directed toward gender equity. The question of why no real progress has been made has permeated conversations for years. Is it implicit bias at the highest levels of organizations? Is there no understanding of the economic benefits of gender equity? Is goal setting similar to quotas, which are sometimes considered a political faux pas? Or is this just too big of a problem? The Institute for Business Value study helps narrow down the three primary reasons organizations have not made this a business priority, and we believe these to be representative of most companies. The following are insights gained through the study.[168]

> Organizations are not convinced that gender equity is positively correlated with the financial performance of the organization. Despite the tremendous amount of research showing the impact, parity is not a priority. The IBM institute's study shows First Movers outperform their competition in each of these four categories: profitability, revenue growth, innovation and employee satisfaction.[169] Profitability – First Movers:

25 percent report outperforming their competition, versus 13 percent for other organizations. Revenue Growth – First Movers: 23 percent report outperforming their competition, versus 13 percent for other organizations.

"Organizations are over-relying on 'good intentions' and applying a laissez-faire approach to diversity, rather than applying t^{he} disciplined focus on operational execution they apply to other aspects of organizational performance." You know what they say about good intentions: Good intentions with a bad approach often produce negative results. One article that stated equality is a choice. Is it really? As competition for customers, revenue and talent increases, and margins decrease, is choice not diminishing? Gender equity must be viewed as an imperative, and organizations must now view it as a corporate social responsibility. We suggest, again, that gender equity must find a more prominent place in the Jamie Dimon-led Business Roundtable's manifesto and the CSR reports of every organization.

Men, who represent the overwhelming majority of senior leaders worldwide, tend to underestimate the magnitude of gender bias in their workplaces. This seems to reinforce the ideas behind "Men are from

Mars, Women are from Venus," a book suggesting men and women think differently, and have unique and distinct emotional needs and communication preferences. John Gray, author of the book, and respected human relationships expert, points out how men and women often overlook these essential differences when dealing with each other in relationships. Although written for love relationships, the principles also apply in business interrelations. Gray later teamed with Barbara Annis, chair of the Women's Leadership Board at Harvard's Kennedy School of Government and a world-renowned expert on workplace gender issues, to co-author "Work with Me: The Blind Spots between Men and Women in Business." While one may not agree with all the authors' assertions, certainly the theory regarding exclusion can shine an educational lamp for men in senior leadership when it comes to understanding a different perspective.

Men matter, and their desire to understand the culture in which they work and lead is essential to accelerating actual change. Following the First Movers path, organizations can calculate cultural bias impact by asking the following questions, which were part of the Institute for Business Value research.

"First Movers make it a point to ensure women are recognized for their value to the business to the same extent as men." says the IBM Institute for Business Value.[170] There are three primary metrics and questions: equity in valuing contributions, identifying women as high performers, and identifying women with high potential at the same rate as men. First Movers perceive the contributions, performance and potential of women within their organizations. At a rate of 97 percent, First Movers value the individual contributions of men and women equally. At a 90 percent rate, First Movers identify women as high performers as often as men, and at 89 percent, First Movers identify women with high potential as often as men.

A cultural environment of resiliency and inclusivity is key to successful outcomes. We are our own biggest threat, and America may be on a collision course. We are not selecting women for leadership roles at a swift enough pace, K-12 education is not producing as many educated graduates, and there is increasing global competition in the areas of education and leadership. These have the potential to combust. One leadership advisory group, BCG Henderson Institute, notes: "To not only cope with the uncertainties of the global economy in the next ten years but gain advantage, leaders much make diversity an urgent priority in their strategy playbook."[171] This requires a culture that is nondiscriminatory, objective and built upon acceptance. Despite the evidence that a diverse workforce results in increased job satisfaction; improved employee retention; and a higher return on sales, investment capital and equity, women continue to be underrepresented in senior leadership positions across organizations of all sizes. It is not solely about gender; it is about bringing the right people on board and ensuring the culture is one in which both men and women can succeed and ultimately advance the organization's leadership strategy. As a collective, the goal is a healthy and inclusive culture.

While writing this book, co-author Christine was asked to join an emerging board of directors for an organization working with the underserved populations of her state. As mentioned earlier, Christine quickly realized she was the only woman at the table. New board members were needed, and although new to the organization, she voiced the need for more gender diversity on the board. Her comments were met with overwhelming support. It was obvious it was an oversight, not an intentional choice. The other men at the table all looked at each other as if to say, "Why didn't we think of that?" Creating an inclusive culture in a board environment is similar to creating an inclusive environment in an organization. Diversity of thought is an element that will propel an organization to succeed, and that cannot happen with just one gender at the boardroom conference table.

Organizational culture plays a key role in the progression of female leaders and particularly their entrée into and their subsequent experience in the C-suite. "Women are doing their part. Now companies need to do their part, too" says the previously introduced McKinsey Management study.

> **"Culture does not change because we desire to change it. Culture changes when the organization is transformed – the culture reflects the realities of people working together every day."**
>
> *Frances Hesselbein, former CEO, Girl Scouts of America; President/CEO, Frances Hesselbein Leadership Forum at the Johnson Institute for Responsible Leadership*

We have been trying to "evolve" for years with training, education and awareness. Pockets are "evolving," but as proven by the statistics we find in our research, the needle is not really moving. "Changing culture and long-established patterns of attitudes/behaviors is among the most difficult attributes and circumstances that can be changed in an organization or in a whole society. Changing culture is required to meet the changing demands of a global society and economy," says the *Harvard Business Review*.[172] An organization that claims differentiation actually needs to be different, looking and behaving differently peer competitors. Differentiation must come through diversity of people able to handle a changing competitive environment. "Diverse companies are better than their more homogenous counterparts at withstanding unanticipated changes and adapting to external threats," notes the BCG Henderson Institute in "Winning the '20s: The Business Imperative of Diversity." As profound as the finding that links grit to individual success, so too is the assertion made in the piece that "Organizational resiliency or grit will be the greatest predictor of their success or failure … taking advantage of diversity within an organization requires the ability to select and amplify the best approaches (to problem solving). When that kind of adaptive mechanism is baked into the environment and operations of the organization, diversity can do its best work."[173]

When organizations have diversity but are not inclusive, they are missing out by not leveraging the diverse talent they have, due to a lack of inclusivity within the culture. There are specific principles and practices that promote an inclusive culture. These are more intentional activities we believe will accelerate the progress while building capabilities and resilience within organizations. The Boston Consulting Group has identified these as enabling factors,[174] and here we have translated them into specific corporate grit actions:

Enabling Factors	Corporate Grit through Anti-coagulative Actions
Participative Leadership	Accountable and engaged leadership in equity holds leaders at the highest level of the organization accountable for increasing gender diversity. Leaders demonstrate and drive the change toward departmental/organizational goals by hiring, coaching and promoting women into executive leadership positions. These executives lead dialogue and discussion on equity performance.
Formal Strategic Re-emphasis on Diversity Led by the CEO	Formal strategic business initiatives led by the executive leadership team: Consider the company's growth/revenue strategy. Where and how are goals articulated? Similarly, integrate gender-equity goals into a formal strategic planning process to include operational oversight (tracking/review) of quarterly metrics and implementation results. The CEO should require such commitment from all key leaders and update the board on a regular basis.

Frequent and Open Communication Among Teams	Building community through shared goals and shared compensation: What happens when organizations tie compensation to workgroup objectives and performance relative to gender equity? What happens when there is shared responsibility, truly a win-win scenario? Again, this is a proven practice for organizations when driving other performance metrics.
Moral Imperative	Creating measures that demonstrate the moral commitment: implementation of metrics that track and measure gender diversity performance at the leadership and organizational levels. Measure levels of voluntary participation and engagement by employees. High-performing teams are internally motivated – having high quality, motivated members with a shared mindset towards diversity.
Fair and Transparent Employment Practices, including Equal Pay	Transformational employment practices: Formulate policies and require gender-diverse applicant and promotional pools. Executive group review of annual compensation, particularly of those in managerial and initial management roles.

"If leaders successfully drive diversity and establish the workplace environment that allows it to thrive, companies will gain the ability to innovate, grow, and withstand the shocks of the coming decade,"[175] suggests the BCG Henderson article.

Promoting an inclusive culture

Companies that invest in and promote an inclusive culture have the opportunity to not only shape the movement of a more inclusive and diverse landscape but also advance their company into the 21st century (although 20 years *into* the 21st century). Investing in culture can mean providing career development planning specific to the women in their organization. For example, General Motors in Detroit "launched a self-paced online learning program in 2017 that delivers monthly leadership skills lessons. More than 5,000 women initially registered for the program and in 2018 the automaker expanded the program to 36 modules with three different learning tracks — emerging leaders, people leaders and executive leadership."[176]

Promoting an inclusive culture could mean that equal career opportunities are highly regarded and offered. Another example of a company vested in cultural inclusion is L'Oréal USA, which "has three employee-driven think tanks focused on recruiting, retaining and advancing women in its executive ranks and those working in IT and other digital functions.

It also hosts an annual executive offsite gathering to discuss developing women and promoting inclusion."[177] These are examples of companies intentionally designing a culture that embraces women in leadership.

Designing a culture with intention around gender equity means that companies that take on this task may have to deal very directly with bias, both conscious and unconscious. Zoe Philippides, who worked at health care company Amgen for a decade in various roles in the company's legal area before becoming the firm's second chief privacy officer in 2015, says, "Whether or not corporations intend to think this way, there may be a set bias of what a person looks like or acts like for more established historical roles that drives selection. For chief Privacy officers, it's more of a blank slate to be filled by the best candidate."[178]

Companies seeking unique ways to invest in their culture can join the ranks of companies who are adapting the "Rooney Rule," which was established by professional football's Dan Rooney head of the league's diversity committee. The rule adopted in 2003 by team owners requires that any team hiring a head coach has to interview at least one "diverse" candidate. In 2009 the rule was expanded to include general manager and executive-level positions within the teams' front office. For a non-sports affiliated organization, it could mean that for any open leadership position open to female application, the hiring manager would be required to interview "x" number of women for the position. One company did just this. Greenhouse, a bi-coastal firm that specializes in talent acquisition software, created a requirement that "half of the final candidates for consideration for an executive position must be women. In the last 24 months, the executive team has gone from 25 percent to 40 percent." Similarly, Pinterest implemented its version of the Rooney Rule requiring that for any open leadership position, at least one minority and one female must be interviewed.

Women make great leaders, executives and C-suite visionaries, outperforming men in similar leadership dimensions, as we have noted throughout the book. Companies with higher female representation in their top tiers outperform others by delivering 34 percent greater return on investment to shareholders. That is a fact. Companies who invest in gender equity, re-shaping their environment, addressing bias and designing their corporate culture intentionally can shift the gender equity issue *and* achieve higher levels of success at the same time.

From the beginning, the goal of this book has been to respect, coalesce and represent best practices; spotlight the latest research from around the globe; identify ways to replicate for a corporation; and ultimately create an algorithm, combining the individual grit of women and gritty tactics of organizations to create the formula for achieving desired success. Grit scales, formulas, and even the "Executive Grit Model" have been formed and socialized, however how is corporate grit redefined, intentionally built and rapidly replicated? The answer came when we were again reviewing the recent work by Thomas Lee and MacArthur "genius" grant winner Duckworth in the *Harvard Business Review* article, "Organizational Grit."[179] The authors reference health care as a leader in addressing such questions; the industry tends to encourage and produce grit among members of its workforce. "While none of these factors have proven to generate any kind of miracle formula, research has found evidence that over any other measurable factor, possessing the quality of grit is the highest predictor of an individual achieving greatness."[236] We believe it to be the same for corporations.

Corporate grit is defined by *Harvard Business Review* contributors Lee and Duckworth (2018) in this excerpt from the authors' study:

> "Creating the right environment can help organizations develop employees with grit. (The idea of cultivating passion and perseverance in adults may seem naive, but abundant research shows that character continues to evolve over a lifetime.) The optimal environment will be both demanding and supportive. People will be asked to meet high expectations, which

will be clearly defined and feasible though challenging. But they'll also be offered the psychological safety and trust, plus tangible resources, that they need to take risks, make mistakes, and keep learning and growing. Gritty teams collectively have the same traits that gritty individuals do: a desire to work hard, learn and improve; resilience in the face of setbacks; and a strong sense of priorities and purpose."[180]

In health care, patients come to depend on the tenacity and passion of doctors to save their lives or the lives of family members. Furthermore, they believe that "in modern medicine, providing superior care has become so complex that no lone practitioner, no matter how driven, can do it all."[238] Great care requires great collaboration and a team made up of gritty clinicians, male and female, who are a reflection of the entire organization or system. For example, Mayo Clinic and Cleveland Clinic are committed to building a gritty organization, so much so that their actions begin with hiring and are centered on patient care.

None of the above reforms, stories or updates mention a pending crisis or opportunity relative to equity in executive leadership roles. Albeit admirable and commendable that corporations are caring, and organizations are both measuring and rating the level of care, none has posed an important question.

Question of inquiry No. 4:

What happens if the Corporate Social Responsibility and the Women on Boards models and the organizations' efforts were merged, creating a reconceptualization of corporate grit, forcing a recasting of specific measures that foster full representation and participation by women in C-suites and the boardroom? What if we were to infuse parity parameters into the joint model that hold corporations responsible and accountable for measurable, meaningful change?

As shared above, this work is not easy, as it will certainly challenge an organization's own perseverance, passion and persistence relative to grit. However, the state of our country, our world and its social and economic future are at risk. Below is a corporate grit model infusing best practices of 2020 Women on Boards and overall corporate responsibility.

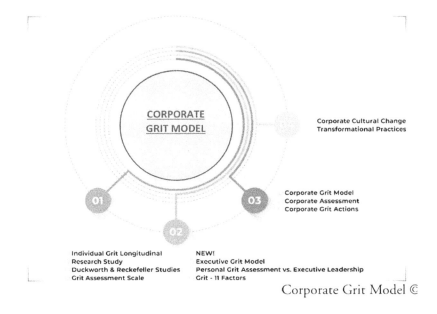

Corporate Grit Model ⓒ

What if the collaboration between the efforts of women seeking advancement and working on their development were networked with an organization's formal efforts to hire, retain and promote women? A more perfect union.

Companies report they are highly committed to gender inclusion, intersectionality, diversity and equity, yet that commitment has not translated into substantial, meaningful progress. Companies may know and understand its importance, but widespread corporate action hasn't been the result of the awareness campaigns. The proportion of women at every level in corporate America has hardly changed. Progress isn't just slow. In some areas it is stalled, in others it is regressed, and in some segments of the population, specifically women with disabilities, the numbers in the C-suite do not even register. To achieve equality, companies must turn good intentions into concrete action.

Another interesting note to consider related to pipeline and availability in corporations is from Sally Blount, dean of the Kellogg School of Management at Northwestern University, and the only woman to lead a top-10 business school. She notes that "data predicts that half or more of the women who earn an MBA this year will drop out of the fulltime work force within a decade. The reasons range from family conflicts to placing less inherent value on position or money. That accounts in part for the low number of women who do reach the very top job, because fewer remain in the pipeline."[181]

Companies report that they are highly committed to gender diversity, yet, that commitment has not translated into meaningful progress. The proportion of women at every level in corporate America has hardly changed.

Collective Grit Model ©

A collective grit model is intended to combine the efforts of individual employees and the organizations in which they work. Peter Grauer, chairman of financial and media giant Bloomberg, says it best: "For me, it's a responsibility. We are all in a war for talent, and that means you have to access underrepresented groups. Together, we can prove outcomes and do a much better job for our stakeholders." The model we advocate in this book seeks to remedy a finding mentioned in the Boston Consulting Group's article, "The Business Imperative of Diversity", "But so far [companies] not only not getting the numbers they need; they're also not gaining as much as they could from the numbers they have … Greater diversity fosters innovation, but it can also strengthen resilience — the capacity to survive the unexpected — which is an equally important weapon heading into the next decade. Diverse companies are better than their more homogenous counterparts at withstanding unanticipated changes and adapting to external threats."[182]

Maximization and optimization of talent will be critical for the 21st century economy and workforce. There have been numerous conversations and completed research regarding how to advance women into key organizational slots. According to the Linkage Advancing Women Leaders published study, "Women leaders perform better, stay at their companies longer and advance in their careers when organizations address four strategic dimensions: Culture, Talent Systems, Focused Leadership Development and Executive Action."[183]

CONSTITUTIONAL GRIT ALGORITHM©

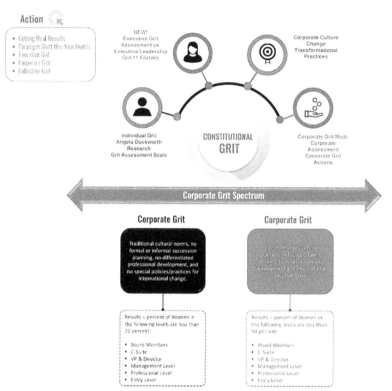

Constitutional Grit Algorithm ©

SUFFRAGE 2.0+:

AN EQUITY ECOSYSTEM AND AWARENESS TO ACTION

OBJECTIVES

Algorithm for full representation and participation by women

Investment 2.0: Equity ecosystem

Ensuring domestic tranquility

CHAPTER 10:
AN ALGORITHM FOR FULL REPRESENTATION AND PARTICIPATION BY WOMEN

It was July 2008 when co-author Toni received her formal, longer-term higher education assignment. She was named assistant dean of the College of Health Sciences at Grand Canyon University in Phoenix, where, at the time, 1,000 students were formal biology majors with aspirations in the fields of medicine, dentistry, physical therapy and others. It was a small, sleepy, unknown institution that began to provide differentiated educational experiences to students that would prove critical to these students from an unbranded institution to earn opportunities at some of the best medical schools in the nation: University of Michigan Medical School, University of Washington, Cornell Veterinary School, and Mayo research internships.

The university's viability and brand would be enhanced if success could be replicated throughout the College of Health Sciences. Within a few years, it was determined that the career and academic pathways offered at GCU, inside and outside of the classroom, were drivers of student success. The ability to predict student performance became more and more critical to aligning and customizing services and interventions based on student type. This same concept can apply to organizations as they develop individualized career paths for employees, creating next generation leaders.

SAS, a leading developer of analytics software, notes in a web article, "How AI Changes the Rules": "Predictive analytics is the use of data, statistical algorithms and machine learning techniques to identify the likelihood of future outcomes based on historical data. The goal is to go beyond knowing what has happened to provide a best assessment of what will happen in the future. Though predictive analytics has been around for decades, it is a technology whose time has come. More and more organizations are turning to predictive analytics to increase their bottom line and competitive advantage."[184]

In the charged spaces of equity and equality we see the integration of analytics into common practices in uncommon ways. Artificial intelligence has been utilized to analyze bias in performance reviews. Katica Roy, an MBA graduate with Hungarian roots, successfully climbing the corporate ladder, until her return from maternity leave. Upon returning to her workplace, she found the environment one of disarray. Her boss had recently been involuntarily released. The restructure had resulted in Roy being assigned two additional teams; her male counterpart was assigned a single team. Roy received no additional compensation for the additional work, while her male colleague was given a raise. After attempts to reconcile the issue amicably, Roy had no choice but to file a formal report with human resources citing the 2009 Lilly Ledbetter Fair Pay Act to receive equal pay for equal work. Not only did she vow to rectify any inequalities within her team, but she went on to create software that would root out bias relative to language and expectations within the performance review process.

Pipeline, a company founded by Roy that deals in the growing industry of diversity and inclusion technology, reported recently that "women tend to receive lower ratings for the same quality of work as men – starting a downward spiral." Roy adds, "They receive less pay, and they're less likely to be put in the leadership pipeline."[185]

These types of disparities in the evaluation process not only lead to greater disparities in pay but also leadership opportunities. When asked what would close the disparity gap, Roy's response was, "The issue needs to be addressed from an economic perspective. CEOs needed to see that it could improve the bottom line". She targeted performance because, while digging into the data of more than 4,000 companies, she found that as gender equity was achieved, organizational revenues increased.[186]

> **"Digging into data from more than 4,000 companies, Roy found that as businesses moved the needle closer to gender equity, their revenue also went up."**
>
> *"Her AI Analyzes Your Performance Review for Gender Bias," Oxymedia.com, Jan. 2020*

Big data is not new to organizations, however it is new to efforts to create equity. Data, big and small has transformed just about every industry in the modern era – manufacturing, technology, finance, education, human resources and now inclusivity. Stacia Garr, founder of RedThread Research, says, "You can have lots of diversity coming into the organization, but if you can't create a place where people feel appreciated and respected, they're not going to stay."[187]

As part of our efforts related to collecting the latest information on data insights related to equity, we included seeking insights from men, either because of their content knowledge or direct experience in building leaders. John was an analytics expert who started his career as a math teacher and transitioned into building pioneering predictive models on a large scale. He would be critical to our conversation for his knowledge of algorithms that replicate successful practices. More importantly, there was the work he had done with his own daughters. First, John spent over a decade building predictive student success, business and other financial models in the education industry. He did so in both booming and tumultuous times. With shrinking margins, increased student attrition and flat enrollment, his work was designed to provide direction to executive leaders, demonstrating ways in which they could improve student outcomes, build programs with unprecedented growth and create economies of scale in the largest portfolio areas of the organization. When asked if it was possible to create an algorithm for women to ascend to the C-suite, John's answer was immediate: "Absolutely."

With unfurled passion, he immediately began naming variables that would potentially go into such an algorithm – experience, education, mindset, tenure in industry, position type, etc. Hurling questions at us faster than we could respond, we quickly arrived at the fact that corporations could also identify high-impact practices that improve equity outcomes. We reviewed the 11 variables identified in the "Top 100 companies for Women to Work For" article and arrived at the concept of "collective grit" as a constructor of multiple parallel pathways that accelerate progress toward the goal. The 11 factors include, among others, mentorship, sponsorship, family supportive policies, current women executive representation, multicultural women representation, female board representation, formal succession planning practices and actual female CEOs.

As noted below, there are very few companies, if any, implementing or diligently pursuing at least six of the 11 high-impact practices. "There is no algorithm needed for that," says John. "But what I would want to understand is what is the make-up of the female population – those eligible to work, versus those not yet at that place. What percent of the women are actually in pursuit of work, and the percent in pursuit of the C-suite?" He then paused, as if he were discovering the answer to the most complex question of all. "Perhaps the gap is in our education of girls at a very early age, in how we are raising them specifically around expectations and goal setting." John has two daughters in their twenties, both successful and on their way to making a great impact on the world. "I simply told them to be the best person you can be but understand the path to getting there."

John asked us if our culture is stifling the female gender or truly helping them develop and be who they want to be. Organizational cultural dynamics are currently being addressed through a myriad effort, all with varying degrees of effectiveness. However, "You can do all of this at the top, but not address where the gap begins … in childhood." Further,

"Is it complacency on the part of the woman or a true bias that stifles ability to maintain the path?" Reflecting upon the high-impact practices/variables and using data to confirm his assessment, John says the one that stood out above the others was mentorship. He notes, "One thing that can accelerate change [is] more expansive and formalized mentorship programs." You change culture through modeling desired behavior. Demonstrated commitment to equity will become of greater importance as this next generation enters corporate America. Says John, "They have no fear of pursuing their dreams and are willing to break through barriers. If you ask my daughter Jess who graduated No. 1 in her law school class, she will identify mentoring, coaching, and support as the foremost impact on her short career." The support needs to begin early to combat damage done before girls can get started. John references an example where Julia, the youngest daughter, and a summa cum laude undergraduate nursing school student, was told her aspirations of a four-year college were too high. Therefore, it is not only an economic but a social and sustainability issue.

So, how can predictive modeling and analytics help? Additional background on John is in order. John started his career as a math teacher, then went into K-12 administration. He made the transition to higher education, eventually becoming assistant dean at a private college where he introduced new ideas and opportunities in the areas of balanced scorecards, business proformas and budgeting and forecasting. This was in 2007, a time when analytics was viewed as a valuable tool in financial-sector success.

However, Educause, a leading educational technology association, had just published an article, "Academic Analytics: A New Tool for a New Era." From the article: "In responding to internal and external pressures for accountability in higher education, especially in the areas of improved learning outcomes and student success, IT leaders may soon become critical partners with academic and student affairs. IT can help answer this call for accountability through academic analytics, which is emerging as a new tool for a new era."[188] Prior to this, the institution John worked for had barely been introduced to analytics, as it had been primarily used in the finance and enrollment areas to predict the number of new students and likely student withdrawals, providing a forecast of quarterly revenues and college needs. John would act as a change agent within the institution and eventually build successful models that would result in significant organizational and student success. Consider another quote from the article that raised the urgency level and presented a profound use case taken from the American Institutes of Research.

"As populations become concerned about their financial well-being and economic security, pressures increase on those individuals and institutions that might influence the outcome. In the information age, one of the most influential institutions is education. And in an era of accountability and liability, organizations that resist pressures for results, accountability and action are suspect. With economic security at stake, how long will society accept that the percentage of the population with a college/university education is stagnant even as the demand has risen, that retention rates have not significantly improved in decades, and that graduates may not have mastered even basic competencies?"[189]

Again, this was 2007; unfortunately, we find ourselves in the same place relative to workforce preparedness and our continued defense of the value of higher education.

Like Angela Duckworth, we reflected with John upon the work that had been done while together at our former institution, work that would center on the student experience and demographic data that would tell the story of their historical academic performance, and how that might indicate future college success. So, high school GPA, highest level of math attainment and prior college credit through dual enrollment were indicators that not only pointed to a level of student preparedness, but these were also where the university began to build programmatic support to increase the probability of semester persistence that would lead to year-over-year retention and, finally, graduation.

John began to describe how one might build a model to evaluate and predict similar success for women seeking advanced leadership roles.

First, the model would have to begin by analyzing women who hold those current positions. Are there consistent experience, education and demographic variables within and across industries? What actionable intelligence might be available if we were to mine the data that is before us? Could that information project a path for millions of women in the workforce who are in pursuit of a career in executive leadership? Some of the data lifted through the qualitative interviews and quantitative information suggests the following factors are critical to the algorithm of individual executive success:

1. Advanced educational degrees – bachelor's to master's, within or outside of the field of study;
2. Multiple departmental assignments throughout an organization – each building and broadening business/ organizational perspective

3. Special projects or assignments that are cross-functional and formed for the purpose of product innovation, large-scale process redesign, or organizational expansion
4. When and where possible, assuming responsibility for global assignments
5. Tenure within an organization culminating in a C-suite position or as a precursor for such a position within an industry competitor
6. The guidance of an organizational sponsor and external mentor/executive coach
7. Executive grit characteristics, especially around cognitive control, executive focus and single mindedness, cross disciplinary planning and operations, and executive productivity.

As suggested earlier, actionable intelligence is used to predict and drive organizational performance. A 2015 *Fortune* article titled "The Algorithmic CEO," notes, "The single greatest instrument of change in today's business world, and the one that is creating major uncertainties for an ever-growing universe of companies, is the advancement of mathematical algorithms and their related sophisticated software. Never has so much artificial mental power been available to so many – the power to deconstruct and predict patterns and changes in everything from consumer behavior to the maintenance requirements and operating lifetimes of industrial machinery."[190]

Question of inquiry No. 5:

If algorithms can help drive "consumer" behavior, can they not also drive corporate behavior relative to building equity? Consider the definition. An algorithm is defined as "a process or set of rules to be followed in calculations or other problem-solving operations," such as solving the long-standing problem of how to advance more qualified women into executive leadership. The chart below encapsulates best practices derived from hundreds of articles and hours of conversations with experts on a corporate framework for accelerating the work of full representation and participation by women in executive leadership.

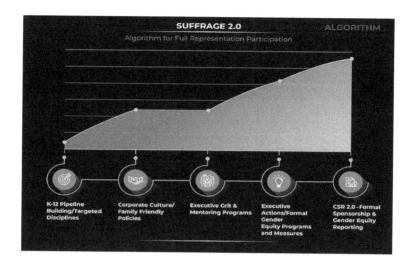

The above Suffrage 2.0 table shows each factor to be considered in the algorithm of full representation and participation. There are five categories in which the 11 activities discussed in 2.0 strategies may have several high-impact practices. No matter the practice, each can be measured by the following:

- Measure 1: Number of female candidates expressing interest in the organization and whether or not that has resulted in an increase in the number of women joining the organization
- Measure 2: Number of promotions for women
- Measure 3: Special projects/high visibility
- Measure 4: Survey results
- Measure 5: Retention

Many organizations build different models around customer loyalty and purchasing trends. Few build such models around their greatest asset: people. Consider these 11 variables identified by diversitywomen.com as ones that should be integrated into a predictive model.

Corporate High-Impact Practices	Ranking
Mentorship	1
Family-friendly policies	2
High percent of managers and/or executives	3
High percent of promotions were women	4
High percent of female executives	5
Succession planning focused on women	6
High female C-suite representation	7
High percent of multicultural women	8
High percent of female employees	9
Female CEOs (+ 2 division presidents)	10
Sponsorship programs	11

Diversity.com

The Diversity.com study was interesting for several reasons, but primarily, for the insights it provides. First, the highest number of impact practices reported by a singular entity was three out of 11, suggesting that there is opportunity for organizations to be more holistic in their approach. Based on the research, scientific calculations and quantitative interviews we have completed for this book, having minimally four of the 11 high-impact practices in place within a company or organization is more likely to accelerate an organization's equal representation in executive-level positions. However, we are still struck by the prediction that it will be another 200 years before equity is achieved.

CHAPTER 11:
INVESTMENT 2.0 - EQUITY ECOSYSTEM

"The world as we have created it is a process of our thinking. It cannot be changed without changing our thinking."

Albert Einstein

"Women are doing their part. Now companies need to do their part, too," notes the McKinsey Management study. Quite frankly, it is time to stop talking and move toward actual transformational efforts with intentional practices and connected actions that create an ecosystem of equity. Many organizations are implementing diversity plans versus integrating creative, equity policies and processes across their enterprise.

Among findings from a Diversity Best Practices offering, "Developing Next Generation of Women Leaders," is this: "Highly effective women are 7x more likely to be found in organizations where executives creatively work to retain female talent. Strategic and decisive action should begin at key points of the pipeline, as the two biggest drivers of the pipeline are hiring and promotions."[191] Women are often disadvantaged in the very beginning of the process, perpetuating disparities in promotion, pay and C-suite representation.

Corporate equity action lab

The corporate culture lab is formed from common interests for organizational and individual team member success. Building of a cross-functional/multidisciplinary team that reviews provided statistical data relative to defined measures/metrics and, more importantly, establishing goals, is critical. Many organizations have culture and diversity committees and even designated diversity positions at the C-suite level. What if that concept could be taken into a lab, a place where equity is structured based on the outcomes of experiments – what works, what does not, what results are achieved and from where?

A successful framework must consider increased competition and organizational threats, as well as other industry environmental trends at all levels of the organization. Experimenting with additions and changes to the framework is also important to produce best results, a formula that works. Organizational drive toward equal representation and participation is a continuous process of improvement and the creation of successful algorithms. A corporate equity lab is structured such that it can take on an opportunity to examine and reverse engineer practices to create an equity framework that addresses each level of the organization.

A corporate culture lab concept is another way that organizations can move the needle from Suffrage 1.0 to 2.0 and act. It establishes, notes *The Globe and Mail's* "5 Factors to Make Your Corporate Culture Effective," "a diverse group of people working in collaboration who can almost always produce a better-quality product than a group that is driven by 'stars.'"[192] Creating labs that are focused on awareness, coupled with accountability, and ensuring an environment in which participants feel comfortable having difficult conversations is imperative. In his article, "Four Ways Company Culture Can Support Women in Leadership," Charles Coy says, "A strong organizational culture begins with education. Provide training and resources that teach employees how to handle topics such as diversity, conflict and bias. Creating an internal dialogue around these often-controversial topics can help make employees aware of unconscious bias and discrimination in the workplace. By providing them with the skills to change behavior you encourage a positive shift in organizational attitude."[193]

Corporate culture labs designed with the intent to improve an organization's inclusion and female representation in executive and C-suite roles has the ability to affect culture in ways a mandate cannot. Coy goes on to say:

"Inclusive cultures emphasize integrity and collaboration and encourage everyone to achieve their potential, while supporting others along the way. One way to do this is through a mentorship program, as such relationships can lead to guidance, opportunity and advice that HR can't always provide.

"Encourage company veterans with 10 or more years of experience in the workplace to identify and sponsor younger rising stars. If your staff skews young, you can also look to outside mentorship resources, such as Everwise, which connects mentors and mentees across organizations. In addition, create measurable diversity and inclusion goals. While most companies track the representation of women, only 44 percent set pipeline targets for gender diversity and even fewer set targets for external hiring and promotions, the McKinsey and LeanIn.org study found.

"Examples of metrics your organization can use are: gender representation of external candidates for hire, assigning sponsors to high potential females in entry level positions, rectify salary differences in comparable positions by gender and create assignments of high-visibility projects by gender."[194]

Examine and reverse engineer the pipeline

The path to greater representation of qualified women in executive leadership can begin in elementary school and lead through higher education to careers, and finally to the C-suites and boardrooms of America. We suggest segmenting the organization into six levels for participation and representation analysis: pre-organization talent pool, entry level, managerial level, leadership, executive leadership/C-suite and board of directors. Each level requires evaluation of the entire talent lifecycle:

- Talent pool interest – Take a cue from the sports industry, any or all of them. Identify top talent early and determine the existing organizational reach: Is it maximizing its relationship with all the educational institutions in the area, including secondary schools and organizations (STEM)?

- Talent pool preparedness – What is the organization's bench strength? Do you have access to well-prepared candidates? Examine post-secondary candidate pool for entry level, internal candidates for lead and managerial roles, and external mentorsphere for leadership/C-suite/board of directors.

- Talent Selection – What are the hiring outcomes at each level: percentage of women hires by position category, newly calculated percentage of women within each organizational band and the newly projected workforce population percentage? Hiring can only be impacted by a couple of crucial efforts: expanding the candidate pool or designating a number of female hires into the organization.

While we are clear that affirmative action comes with both pros and cons, it is even more so that modernizing those efforts has the potential to benefit corporate America culturally, economically, innovatively and socially. Therefore, building a pipeline strategy entails increasing the number of women in entry-level leadership positions.

Challenge: Although women earn more bachelor's degrees than men, they are less likely to be hired into entry-level jobs. This requires a nontraditional approach to talent pool development. Reverse engineering may include designating a top female and male leader to act as dual designers to work with community assets for the identification and development of talent. Using key data elements for each pipeline level to reverse engineer your systems for optimal outcomes is another opportunity to ensure a greater level of equity.

Solution: University-corporate pipeline collaboratives are one solution to the pipeline challenge. Every university/college has a career center, typically underfunded and under-resourced, which could benefit from the infusion of corporate financial and human assets designated specifically to build a network for pipeline development. A number of such efforts exist, and best practices include the following:

- Start by examining current pipeline performance measures against goals: number of women employees and the number of interviews conducted to obtain that number of employees, number of current open positions and the projected change to the overall workforce population percentage if positions are filled by women.

- Expand disciplines in which women are recruited for entry-level positions.

- Provide female STEM students a corporate mentor during these young learners first year in college. This helps universities with retention and supports organizations by expanding the candidate pool.

- Add a corporate advisor to strengthen the student's connection with and positive perception of the company.

- Integrate meaningful, hands-on internships into career development strategies. Hold career advisors accountable for placement and retention progress.

- Commit to hiring young talent *before* student graduation.

Improving the pipeline through promotion

Challenge: At the first critical step, and continuing through managerial roles, the gender disparity grows further. Women are less likely to be hired into manager-level jobs, and they are far less likely to be promoted into them. Largely because of these gender gaps, men end up holding 62 percent of manager positions, while women hold only 38 percent," says a LeanIn offering titled "The Broken Rung Keeping Women from Management."[195] In this latest collaboration between McKinsey and LeanIn, the organizations' research states: "… Researchers find that the biggest obstacle for women occurs at one of the very first steps on the corporate ladder — the initial promotion to management. Men are far more likely than women to be promoted from their entry-level jobs to manager, and this early inequity also explains why they are fewer women at senior levels of management — women just cannot ever catch up."

For their fifth annual report on women in the workplace, McKinsey and LeanIn surveyed 329 companies and questioned more than 68,500 employees. The study found that for every 100 men promoted or hired at the manager level, only 72 women received the same promotion. The gender difference is so great that the researchers claim this "broken rung" at the first step to manager is the biggest obstacle that women face on the path to leadership. In fact, the broken rung at the bottom of the corporate ladder also keeps women from reaching the top of the ladder. Since fewer women are promoted to junior management, there are fewer women in the pipeline when it comes time to choose employees for senior management roles. As a result, the number of women decreases at every subsequent management level."[196]

Solution: Kim Elsesser, senior editor for *Forbes* says there are ways to resolve and solve for the broken rung women experience:

> "Fortunately, there are remedies for organizations committed to reducing this gender bias. The LeanIn/McKinsey report highlights success stories at NextRoll, Nordstrom and Sodexo. After prioritizing gender diversity, NextRoll increased the number of women in senior management from 27 percent to 40 percent, Nordstrom increased the share of women in the C-Suite from 7 percent to 40 percent, and Sodexo has increased the number of women by more than 20 percent at the SVP level.
>
> "What is the secret to this success? The specifics at each company varied and included strategies like setting targets and keeping managers accountable. But all three organizations had one thing in common—commitment to improving gender diversity."[197]

Talent systems

Highly effective women leaders are two times more likely to be found in organizations with fair, people-related decision-making processes. In his article, "How Growth-Minded CEOs Operate their Talent Management Systems," John Lankford asks and answers the following: "What do high-performing companies have in common? Their senior leaders actively focus on, participate in and refine their systems for finding, keeping, and growing great employees."[198] What is most revealing about Lankford's article is the level of specificity used in addressing the entire career cycle of women. Lankford, a four-time winner of the prestigious North American Business Advisor of the Year award who counts more than two decades in corporate executive leadership responsibilities, provides the reader a business case for employee engagement at an early level, but also laments that still today there are those leaders choose not to take advantage of the integrated talent management system comprised of unique efforts said to be inextricably linked to the organization's ability to attract top talent and outperform the competition in the areas of recruiting, hiring and selection, onboarding, training and development, accountability, leadership development, promotion of talent, compensation and measuring culture. More important than an awareness of these documented systems is putting them in place following through with full execution.

Focused leadership development for women

An organization will never outperform its leadership team. The Center for Creative Leadership reports, "Successful organizations realize that simply waiting for culture and systems to change is not enough. For women leaders to grow, companies must differentially invest in their leadership development above and beyond what is typical for all leaders." Organizations approach development efforts differently; some are external to the organization, while others are internal yet informal. What, unfortunately can be consistent in the approach is the lack of illumination upon the "path" to the C-suite. What if the ambiguity were removed and women were given specific roles with specific outcomes, the very recommendation from "Advancing Women Leaders," a piece posted by executive training solutions company Linkage. "Women leaders are 7x more likely to be highly engaged if they are encouraged to take on growth opportunities. Women who believe in future promotion opportunities are 16x more likely to be in a company where women receive consistent feedback."[199] Successful organizations understand the importance of building competencies to advance and promote women leaders. Formal programs and experiences, high-visibility opportunities, stretch assignments within and outside of the organization, and feedback and coaching to build self-awareness are primary domains for development.

Commit to a target

Many companies set diversity/equity goals based on where they stand currently or on past performance. Reverse engineering approaches goal setting differently, as targets are set based on the actual equity percentage.

Consider the following before committing:

Within your organization, what does the data indicate? What are your actual gender diversity numbers by department? What is the industry average? Your competitors – what is the representation of female leadership, are there creative recruitment and retention strategies? The chart below depicts a data snapshot of this information.

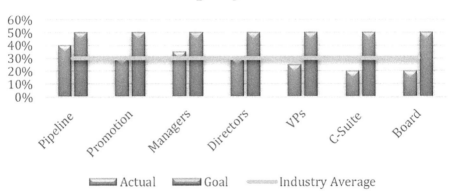

Denise Cautela, a marketing change agent and community builder who heads LinkedIn's North America customer engagement efforts, shares in her recent "3 Ways to Promote

Gender Diversity in the C-Suite" that companies with a greater number of C-suite women tend to have a workforce that is predominantly women. "If your organization has 41 percent female employee base, the organization is more likely to have C-suite women. Further, if a workforce is 34 percent or below, it tends to have no female executives," says Cautela.[200] What is the percentage of women in your current workforce? Is your commitment at 50 percent? If that same mathematical concept were to be applied to entry level, managerial, executive and board positions, is the organization minimally at 50 percent?

Commit to an enhanced sponsorship and mentorship program

Executive sponsors who are poised to promote female leaders and sponsor them throughout the path to the C-suite need to have some very specific tools in place in order to truly encourage transformation and drive social change. Specifically, in your organization, which of your executive sponsors are prepared to mentor and coach leaders to drive strategy, innovation and growth at an enterprise-wide level? Are they armed with the development mindset and capabilities necessary to identify those who will one day succeed them in their executive-level role? Are they able to empower their teams and leaders to transform culture to accelerate business strategy? And are they prepared to foster socially conscious, purpose-driven leaders?

A recent Center for Talent Innovation survey of more than 3,200 college-educated employees who work in white-collar jobs found that 71 percent of those who identified as sponsors reported their protege was the same race or gender as their own. This built on past research that found 58 percent of women and 54 percent of men admitted to choosing a protege because they "make me feel comfortable."[201] Although many companies are trying to improve diversity, Jena McGregor, *Washington Post* author of the article "Nearly Three-Quarters of Executives Pick Proteges Who Look Just Like Them" says, "Our unconscious biases draw us to people like ourselves. Even after years of speaking about the power of diversity, one never knows when he or she will be called to be the voice of change."[202]

We make a distinction between mentors and sponsors who specifically advocate for and aid a person's promotion within a company. Often this is a CEO, a board member or another lead executive who helps make specific role assignments. An effective sponsorship and mentorship program should incorporate the following:

- Active promotion of upcoming qualified women — several women, not just one — and advocacy on their behalf to peers and board members.
- Encouragement of women to research and consider networking opportunities that provide them with valuable connections with like-minded professionals.
- Provision of meaningful and hands-on opportunities to work with boards, media and company stakeholders.
- Clear, detailed discussions centered on performance expectations, measurements and outcomes with female employees moving into executive leadership roles.

Below, our "Mentorsphere" model is a mentoring impact model, which provides an opportunity for organizations to assess their mentorship effectiveness. Purposeful mentoring that leads to increased board seat and C-suite equity should be the goal of all corporate programs. Often, well-intentioned efforts do not result in change. How often does your organization evaluate the inclusivity of its existing C-suite or review personal circles of influence and the opportunity to leverage those relationships for increased representation and participation by women?

The Personal Mentorsphere – Who's in your Circle?

Circle of Responsibility + Inclusivity = Impact

The Mentorsphere model suggests that time spent mentoring is on purpose and for purpose, impacting longstanding disparities to bring forth a new Era of Equity.

The Goal: Cross-sector equity pipeline development and placement

1. What is the make up of your mentorsphere?
2. Is the approach to mentoring similar or different for men and women?
3. How do you leverage mentoring to create equity within your industry? Is inclusivity possible within your industry?
4. Who advocates for women leaders within your sphere of influence?
5. What methods are most effective in successfully diversifying the most inner circle of an organization?
6. Reputation as a source for diversity/inclusivity?
7. How do you measure the impact of your mentoring - Number of referrals and placements?

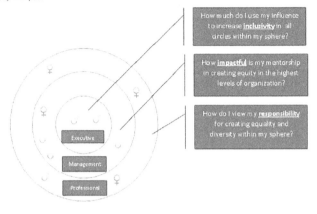

As a mentor creating the greatest amount of impact, take a look at 10 mentees, who are they and what levels of leadership are represented/underrepresented?

The Corporate Mentorsphere – Who's in the inner Circle?

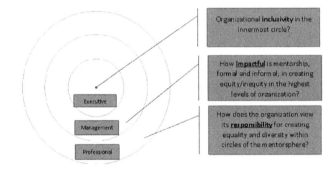

Commit through policy changes and transparency

Policy changes are potential game-changers for organizations that have not invested in internal reforms related to diversity and inclusion. Organizations like As You Sow, a nonprofit leader in shareholder advocacy, have created an interesting model to affect gender equity change across the financial services industry. Gabe Rissman writes for *asyousow.org*:

"Many mutual fund managers now make the argument that gender pay parity, in addition to board diversity, is essential to corporate performance. The campaign began in 2014, with Arjuna Capital's shareholder proposal for eBay to close its gender pay gap. Though it only received support from eight percent of shareholders, the next year, support grew to 51 percent, and eBay committed to pay parity the day of the vote. The campaign took off. Over the last four years, 10 different investor groups have engaged with at least 47 companies, asking them to report on their policies and goals to reduce any gender pay gap, earning commitments from more than 20 companies, including Apple, Bank of America, and Amazon to analyze and disclose these gaps.

"As the gender pay equality movement has grown, it has become clear that access to jobs and a fair chance at promotion are crucial inputs to solving the gender pay gap. Shareholders have increasingly pressed companies to explain how they ensure equal access to employment for women and minorities. Walden and Trillium Asset Management have led the charge by filing dozens of shareholder proposals over the past few years, persuading a number of companies in the retail and financial services sectors to disclose equal opportunity statistics."[203]

Commitment to cultural shift

True change will require a holistic, corporate-wide approach. Until there is cultural change within and throughout an organization, outdated and primitive ideas like "the old boys' club," "frat boy" mentalities, outdated and unfair stereotypes about women's leadership abilities, and men stuck in another time and unwilling to recognize and treat women as equals will continue to impede women's advancement. This requires recognizing and acting on the value of diversity and inclusion in the 21st-century workplace. Cultural shifts typically take time, so how do we expedite the process? It will require a whole new level of corporate grit. There is no easy way to begin annihilating stereotypes and reshaping thinking relative to the appreciation and optimization of talent, regardless of gender. Therefore, doing everything possible to position people for success and building/sharing best practices is critical.

Stereotypes

The website *econsultancy.com*, in a posting titled "How Brands are Fighting Against Gender Stereotypes," offers this: "According to Czech brand Aurosa, beer is a beverage that can only be enjoyed by men. Why else would they have created the ground-breaking new concept of beer for women – a product designed to 'prove that women can succeed anywhere without having to adapt and sacrifice their natural femininity.'"[204] What? Since when do women need an alcoholic beverage that only they might enjoy?

Katherine B. Coffman of the *Harvard Business Review* writes, "Gender stereotypes distort our views of both ourselves and others — and that may be especially troubling for women, since buying into those stereotypes could be creating a bleak self-image that is setting them back professionally." Coffman, as assistant professor of business administration at Harvard, continues, "This work suggests a need for structuring group work/decision-making in a way that recognizes the most talented members for their contributions despite gender stereotypes. Stereotypes are pervasive, widely-held views that shape beliefs about our own and others' abilities, likely from a very young age … Until we can change these stereotypes, it's essential to think about how we can better inoculate individuals from biases induced by stereotypes, helping people to pursue fulfilling careers in the areas where their passions and talents lie." [205]

Stereotypes can potentially lead or show up in the organization as conscious or unconscious bias, and therein lies one of the issues we have been discussing in this book. Awareness is necessary, investment is crucial and culture change is the final puzzle piece in completing an organization's transformation toward gender equality at all levels.

> **"People transfer power to others who make them feel comfortable."**
>
> *Jena McGregor, Washington Post reporter on corporate management and business trends*

Case study: Ernst & Young

The pursuit of equal representation is futile without creating equitable circumstances within the culture of which sponsorship is at the core. Earnst & Young's efforts in this arena have included addressing inequities of access to executive-level roles by looking at the level – when existent – of "mentors and sponsors, internal and external networks, and developmental experiences that would get them to the next level. While women are highly mentored, they are not highly sponsored," according to Andrea Ramsey, director of global and America's diversity and inclusiveness at EY.[206] Many businesses have found success by building boards of directors designed to help "convert" women leaders into partners, typically assisting in broadening experiences, not skill development. Another critical element is the insurance of appropriate networks, the basis for EY's Inclusiveness Leadership Program, a multiyear program that pairs select high-potential partners and principals with a coach and a member of the America's office executive committee. To further demonstrate the criticality of sponsorship, EY launched a webcast specifically guiding women on how to seek and leverage sponsorships.

Sponsorships for women across all races and ethnicities are also a critical factor in solving for gender inequity. In the book, "Breaking Through: The Making of Minority Executives in Corporate America," authors David Thomas and John Gabarro pose the question that lies at the heart of achieving gender equality in the C-suite: "What are the most significant factors in an organization's ability to sustain its diversity efforts over time and achieve racial integration at all levels of the hierarchy?" While numerous studies have been conducted to answer this question, Ann Morrison's benchmark work in studying leading companies answers the question this way: "The involvement of executives and senior managers is a crucial driver."[207]

While our findings point to the importance of leadership, like Morrison, we found that leadership support and commitment is not enough, regardless of race or ethnicity. You can simply look at a brief definition to distinguish support from involvement. "Support" is defined as "give assistance to, especially financially; enable to function or act." Conversely, "involvement" is the fact or condition of being involved with or participating in something. Involvement also implies emotional or personal association, demonstrating a completely different level of investment.

Commit to invest – Organizational exemplars

Diversity.com is an organization focused on the empowerment of women by providing exemplars and education, tools that are intended for self-assessment. Most important is the site's list of "Best 100 Companies for Women's Leadership Development." The work being done within these companies deserves recognition and replication. Each has adopted components of the corporate grit model and appears to be building toward a fully integrative model that addresses all aspects of leadership development.

Companies included on the diversity.com list were evaluated based on "women's upward mobility, proportion of multicultural women on staff, presence of female managers and executives, presence of women on the company's board, mentorship programs for women, family-friendly policies, and inclusion of women in succession planning."[208]

Our corporate grit model emphasizes bringing greater gender equality in corporate management culture practiced by the most senior leaders, ensuring practices that facilitate and promote innovation and communication up, down and throughout the organization. These create transparency, openness and the generation of ideas across the enterprise. When aligning these to practices with those companies highlighted on *diversity.com's* top 100 list, family-friendly policies emerge as a core component. Out of the earlier-discussed 11 Diversity Women criteria, family friendly policies ranked 2nd, as 37 percent of the organizations were found to have such policies. Some of the most notable are below.

- AT Kearney, a global management consulting firm, has implemented programs and policies that support work-life balance. Pathways for Parents has launched a program that allows parents one year to reacclimate, and another company, WorkSmart, provides employee teams with the ability to determine their own travel times and how much they will travel for work-related business. Wyndham Hotels & Resorts surveys its customer base of women to improve clients' experience, create nuances in services and products, and to launch a "Women on Their Way" program. Now with 18 chapters and 2,500 members, it has expanded to career support programming.

- CA Technologies provides work-from-home opportunities to employees; 30 percent of employees telecommute full- time.
- Finnegan offers flexible work schedules, robust parental leave pay and benefits, and backup childcare support for employees.
- MetLife offers employees parental leave coaching and flex-time opportunities utilized by 96 percent of its employees.
- Novartis Pharmaceuticals offers up to $10K annual tuition assistance to qualifying employees.
- SC Johnson Consumer Goods has created summer programs, educational sessions for teens and daycare opportunities.

There is no better investment in organizational resources than the development and preparation of a business' people. Pipeline building must begin with younger women, even young girls, through K-12 outreach programs that reach across socioeconomic, demographic, and academic boundaries.

To retain and maximize talent within an organization, the same efforts must occur. Diversity Women rankings bear this out, identifying three of the 11 measures that correlate with the Suffrage 2.0 Investment strategy: mentoring, succession planning and sponsorship. While mentoring showed strong support, identified by 50 percent of the listed organizations as a key highlight, succession planning (6 percent) and sponsorship (1 percent) represented areas of significant opportunity. This is most concerning, given these are arguably the two ways in which high-performing women are propelled from management positions to the C-suite. Below are examples of elite, noteworthy companies getting it right.

State Farm Financial Services has a Leadership Development Acceleration Program. Ernst & Young consulting services is the only organization where a formal sponsorship program is mentioned, with 50 Professional Women's Network chapters across the U.S. and Canada. Similarly, six of 100 companies reported succession planning as an important aspect of female development. Bristol-Myers Squibb has a formal executive mentoring process in which senior managers are partnered with junior executives, women and people of color to accelerate their growth and careers. In 2013, Cisco initiated efforts to accelerate succession planning for female vice presidents and senior directors. The company now reports that "75 percent of the senior vice presidents on the leadership team of the finance group are women."[209]

Other examples can be found:

- Wyndham Hotels & Resorts has developed mentoring one-on-one programs and circles for targeted "difficult-to-recruit" roles such as IT and women of color. These efforts not only focus on pipeline building but also retention of talent once successfully recruited.

- Kaiser Permanente is a health care company whose workforce diversity is such that there is no majority group. Kaiser has established a National Diversity Agenda, which has resulted in greater gender-equality: Half its physicians and executives are women, and 35 percent of its board members are women.

- Kaiser has launched diverse employee mentorship opportunities and access to affinity groups and special focus groups.

- Texas Instruments, a global semiconductor manufacturer has contracted with a recruiting firm to ensure boardroom diversity among its 11-member board to female, Hispanic and African-American representation. TI Diversity Network is an employee-led diversity effort that features educational programs, career development and volunteer projects.

- Principal Financial Group has created Women's Network for Leaders, including an executive sponsor, designed to move women into leadership through career development, networking, job shadowing and mentoring.

- Finnegan, Henderson, Farbow, Garret & Dunner is an intellectual property law firm with a technical and science competency. Defying traditional law firm leadership, FHFG&D is comprised of 55 percent women who are staff chief officers, and 71 percent are at management and supervisory levels. The firm has also launched a Women's Initiative program focused on employee mentoring.

- Eli Lilly & Company is a global pharmaceutical firm with a formal succession planning process that has resulted in management representation of 36 percent women and 29 percent female board representation. Global Lilly Women's network includes 4,500 members across the world and helps women successfully lead and exert influence at the company.

Organizations measure what matters. Seven of the 11 Diversity Women components are measures of female representation and participation in management and board seats. They includ the percentage of female/managers, board members, female CEOs, multicultural women, female employees and female executives. Some of the highlighted accomplishments:

- Prudential Financial has in place two divisional presidents and 33 percent of senior managers are women.

Constitutional Grit | 233

- Salesforce's CEO has a stated goal to create a 50 percent female workforce, and the company's top 20 women earn more than the top 20 men.
- Walmart has seen a 92 percent increase in female market managers over the past five years.
- Wells Fargo has a 16-member board of directors; 31.25 percent are female and "almost all top-two-level executives participate in a cross-cultural mentoring program."
- Principal Financial Group has reported that half of the company's most recent promotions went to women in a traditionally male-dominated industry. One-third of the executive-level positions are held by women. Additionally, 36 percent of PFG's board seats are filled by women, compared to 18 percent within the financial industry.

CHAPTER 12:
ENSURING DOMESTIC TRANQUILITY

The U.S. has an unprecedented opportunity to invest in women and gender parity in a meaningful and measurable way, an opportunity that – when achieved – will resolve the lack of women in the country's C-suites and boardrooms. Throughout this book, we have not minimized the challenges and obstacles, yet we are boldly confident that with intentionality, action and focus, we can overcome these challenges and evolve into a generation of trailblazers for those who follow in our footsteps. There's momentum that has been generated – however slowly – since Suffrage 1.0. Women continue to shape society, making significant contributions to local and national economies, whether in the public or private sector. Women contribute to the global economy as a collective force, and the world is paying attention.

At the time of the first printing of this book, Google announced that it would be awarding $1 million to partner organizations to increase the representation of women in technology communities around the world. The company is championing women because it recognizes, as reported by

Marketwired, "women-led tech companies achieve 35 percent higher ROI than their male counterparts." Investing in gender parity will not only shape this generation and those who come after us, but it will reshape the societal norms to which we have become accustomed. Instead of conscious and unconscious bias clouding a C-suite or board seat determination, qualifications and a commitment to diversity will take precedence over gender.

"As of 2019, gender-equitable and inclusive development is one of the Sustainable Development Goals (SDGs) of the United Nations, with Goal number 5 focused on realizing gender equality and empowering all women and girls. These objectives are also reflected in the strategic blueprint 'ASEAN 2025: Forging Ahead Together' and made more achievable through technological changes brought by the Fourth Industrial Revolution."[210] With such a goal – laid out by an international body of government leaders in such concise terms – there exists a never-before-in-history opportunity to replace ideas and conversation with meaningful and actionable results. It will take action – action that begins with changing a culture of pre-determination and gender bias, action that results in a culture shift so dramatic the next generation may indeed wonder what all the fuss was about. It will require action that creates the path forward in this country and around the world, leading us to gender equality without that is accepted by all as the norm.

While preparing for the 2nd edition of this book, we were asked by the Plus Alliance Annual Conference leadership to lead a corporate working group at its 2020 meeting, "Providing Leadership Pathways for Women." Normally, the annual conference is held in person in a host country, but due to the coronavirus pandemic, the meeting was staged virtually. In collaboration with London Kings College and University of New South Wales in Australia, we embarked upon a month-long conference, meeting weekly with a group of approximately 15 women. Each week we explored how to diversify existing opportunities provided to women in academia and industry, accessing some of the greatest minds and latest research. At the end of the conference, we developed a model that the women approved for use in addressing gender-equity issues and solutions. Our model featured a four-part design that included Preparation, Position, Promotion and Placement. This proprietary four-part design template was used to incorporate the recommended activities that would drive increased pathways for women seeking to advance in leadership.

Washington State University recently published a blog about women joining the ranks of C-suite positions. Included was the following:

"Women have made many leadership gains on their own, but they shouldn't have to do so completely unsupported. In fact, businesses can help their female employees reach the C Suite in at least three ways: *Forbes* recommended increasing the number of female board members.

"Female employees who see more women in the boardroom are better inspired to pursue open executive-level positions. Gallup pointed out that children could be a primary factor in a woman's decision to work. It is no secret that women are generally the primary caregivers, and this fact compromises many women's ability to achieve their full potential at work.

"Businesses that want to increase their number of female executives should make sure these positions provide an adequate work-life balance or at least have some sort of family care benefits. Such initiatives benefit men as well, giving them more time and capability to raise their children. Businesses that want higher profits, greater female representation, and a greater portion of women achieving their full potential can create corporate initiatives to achieve such ends."[211]

In early 2019, the International Labor Organization published the article "Women in leadership bring better business performance," which included the following from Deborah France-Massin, a senior manager in the UN system with more than 20 years' experience in labor and social affairs at national, European and international levels: "The business case for getting more women into management is compelling. In an era of skill shortages, women represent a formidable talent pool that companies are not making enough of. Smart companies who want to be successful in the global economy should make genuine gender diversity a key ingredient of their business strategy. Representative business organizations and employer and business membership organizations must take a lead, promoting both effective policies and genuine implementation."[212]

We couldn't agree more.

The Center for Creative Leadership posted an article, "How to Propel More Women into The C Suite." The author, John Ryan says, "Create cultures that sponsor women leaders. Data suggests that women are less likely to raise their hands for bigger roles and that they are more likely to be passed over for men whose potential is perceived to be greater, even when women are better qualified. So, their bosses need to be much more proactive in helping women identify and act on potential promotions – and in advocating for them throughout the hiring process. Ultimately, this is about changing organizational cultures in support of gender diversity, and senior executives are best positioned to lead that effort."[213]

Dave McKay, president and CEO of Royal Bank of Canada, says "We know that fully realizing the talents of the many, not the few, is the route to true business success and sustainable growth.

"There is no magic formula to achieve gender diversity, much less systematically provide opportunities for women to take on senior leadership roles," McKay continues. "Ambitious organization-wide diversity programs have had limited success, largely because they are not tailored to particular circumstances and lack serious support and commitment from top management. Companies may want to consider the following actions as they move forward with their women's leadership process":[214]

Follow the leaders. Companies that are having the most success with their female talent development initiatives tend to have certain characteristics in common: an open and inclusive mindset, flexibility and a willingness to accept and support change at all levels of the organization. The leaders we have interviewed and those we have included in this book exhibit these attributes. Their common focus is forward movement. It is important for organizations to strive to go beyond their current policies and procedures. Looking ahead and staying focused on new ideas and new ways to close the gender gap are vital to accelerate women's professional advancement. Companies are much more likely to achieve success when they adopt the principle of "continuous innovation," focusing on continual improvements, thinking creatively and implementing fresh initiatives to achieve gender diversity at all levels of management. They must establish accountability. Ultimately, senior leaders are rewarded not for good intentions but for results. If key leaders are given specific financial or other targets, and rewards when meeting their targets, they are much more likely to make active efforts to develop and advance women leaders – and to meet corporate goals for financial performance.

Our goal from the initial research launch has been to bring together the latest information in collaboration with industry best practices and newly developed models that provide a roadmap for the individual and the collective.

Now it is your turn. Culture shift awaits, and your action is the next step. A generation is waiting.

FURTHER READING

The U.S. Constitution Bill of Rights

Women's Suffrage Movement

"Grit" by Angela Duckworth

"Three Feet from Gold" by Sharon Lechter

"Succeeding through Doubt, Fear and Crisis" by Deborah Bateman

END NOTES

1. Delli Carpini, M. X., & Williams, B. A. (1993). The Year of the Woman? Candidates, Votes and the 1992 Elections. Political Science Quarterly, 108 29-36. Retrieved from http://repository.upenn.edu/asc_papers/22

2. Cooney, R. (2005). The University of Vermont, Center for Cultural Pluralism (2020). *100th Anniversary of Women's Suffrage Power, Privilege, & the Vote: Focus on Women Culture & Herstories of Suffrage.* https://www.uvm.edu/ccp/100th-anniversary-womens-suffrage-power-privilege-vote-focus-women-culture-herstories-suffrage

3. Rosenzweig, J. (2019). *Four Reasons Women Still Struggle to Advance to and in the C-Suite.* HR Technologist. https://www.hrtechnologist.com/articles/diversity/four-reasons-women-still-struggle-to-advance-to-and-in-the-csuite/

4. Peck, A. (Sept. 2008). Costco Connection. *Grit.* http://www.costcoconnection.com/connection/201809?pg=47#pg47

5. Duckworth, A. (2016). *Grit: The power of passion and perseverance.* Scribner/Simon & Schuster.

6. Bailey, N. (2018). What's Better than Grit? Reading Books and a Good Teacher. https://dianeravitch.net/2018/09/10/nancy-bailey-whats-better-than-grit-reading-books-and-a-good-teacher/

7. National Women's History Project. (2020, August). How Women Won the Vote. https://nationalwomenshistoryalliance.org/wp-content/uploads/gazette_How-Women-Won-Vote-.pdf

8. Walker, B., Soule, S. (2017, June). Changing Company Culture Requires a Movement, Not a Mandate. *Harvard Business Review.* https://hbr.org/2017/06/changing-company-culture-requires-a-movement-not-a-mandate

9. Warner, J., Ellmann, N. and Boesch, D. (2018). The Women's Leadership. Center for American Progress. https://www.americanprogress.org/issues/women/reports/2018/11/20/461273/womens-leadership-gap-2/

10. Warner, J., Ellmann, N. and Boesch, D. (2018). The Women's Leadership. Center for American Progress. https://www.americanprogress.org/issues/women/reports/2018/11/20/461273/womens-leadership-gap-2/

11. Miller, C. (2018). The Number of Female Chief Executives is Falling. *New York Times*. https://www.nytimes.com/2018/05/23/upshot/why-the-number-of-female-chief-executives-is-falling.html

12. Mejia, Z. (21 May 2018). Just 24 female CEOs lead the companies on the 2018 Fortune 500 – fewer than last year. CNBC. https://www.cnbc.com/2018/05/21/2018s-fortune-500-companies-have-just-24-female-ceos.html

13. Desilver, D. (30 April 2018). Women scarce at top of U.S. business – and in the jobs that lead there. https://www.pewresearch.org/fact-tank/2018/04/30/women-scarce-at-top-of-u-s-business-and-in-the-jobs-that-lead-there/

14. Krivikovich, A., Nadeau, M., Robinson, K., Starikova, I., and Yee, L. (2018). Women in the Workplace 2018. https://www.mckinsey.com/featured-insights/gender-equality/women-in-the-workplace-2018

15. Atkins, B. (7 August 2018). Where Did All the Female CEOs Go? Forbes. Where Did All The Female CEOs Go? (forbes.com)

16. Posner, M. (7 March 2019). Why It's So Important to Close the Female Leadership Gap. Forbes. Why It's So Important To Close The Female Leadership Gap (forbes.com)

17. Toy, A. (June 2019). Implicit Bias and the Gender Leadership Gap. Marquette University Law School Faculty Blog. https://law.marquette.edu/facultyblog/2019/06/implicit-bias-and-the-gender-leadership-gap/

18. Warner, J., Corley, D. (21 May 2017). The Women's Leadership Gap: Women's Leadership by the Numbers. Center for American Progress. https://www.americanprogress.org/issues/women/reports/2017/05/21/432758/womens-leadership-gap/

19. Catalyst. (2019). List: Women CEOs of the S&P 500. https://www.catalyst.org/research/women-ceos-of-the-sp-500/

20. Rabouin, D. (22 May 2019). Slow progress for women CEOs. Retrieved from https://www.axios.com/women-ceos-incoming-rates-2018-worldwide-1c8d221c-4978-45b2-a011-89583b2d4ae3.html

21. Blumberg, Y. (2 March 2018). Companies with more female executives make more money – here's why. Retrieved from https://www.cnbc.com/2018/03/02/why-companies-with-female-managers-make-more-money.html

22. Blumberg, Y. (2 March 2018). Companies with more female executives make more money – here's why. Retrieved from https://www.cnbc.com/2018/03/02/

why-companies-with-female-managers-make-more-money.html

23. McKinsey & Company – Desvaux, G. Devlllard, S. (2008). Women Matter 2: Female leadership, a competitive edge for the future. https:// www.mckinsey.com/~/media/ McKinsey/Business percent20Functions/Organization/Our percent20Insights/Women percent20matter/Women_matter_ oct2008_english.ashx

24. Lean In, McKinsey & Company. (2019). Women in the Workplace 2019. Retrieved from https://wiw-report.s3.amazonaws. com/Women_in_the_Workplace_2019.pdf

25. Huang, J. Krivkovich, A. Starikova, I., Yee, L., and Zanoschi, D. (30 Sept. 2020). Women in the Workplace 2019. Retrieved from https://www.mckinsey.com/featured-insights/gender-equality/women-in-the- workplace-2019

26. Warner, J., Corley, D. (21 May 2017). The Women's Leadership Gap: Women's Leadership by the Numbers. https://www. americanprogress.org/issues/women/reports/2017/05/21/432758/womens-leadership-gap/

27. McKinsey & Company – Desvaux, G. Devlllard, S. (Oct. 2008). Women Matter 2: Female leadership, a competitive edge for the future. https://www.mckinsey.

com/~/media/McKinsey/Business%20Functions/ Organization/Our%20Insights/Women%20matter/ Women_matter_oct2008_english.ashx

28. Byham, T. (2020). Women CEOs Highest Representation on the Fortune 500 list Isn't Enough. Forbes. https://www.forbes.com/sites/forbescoachescouncil/2020/08/03/women-ceos-highest-representation-on-the-fortune-500-list-still-isnt-enough/?sh=2d6751715aa8

29. Hinchliffe, E. (2020). Women Run 37 Fortune 500 Companies, A Record High. Fortune. https://fortune.com/2020/05/18/women-run-37-fortune-500-companies-a-record-high/

30. Lean In. (2018). 2018 Women in the Workplace. https://leanin.org/women-in-the-workplace-report-2018/men-still- outnumber-women-at-every-level

31. U.S. Bureau of Labor Statistics. (2019). Labor Force Statistics from the Current Population Survey. Retrieved from https://www.bls. gov/cps/cpsaat11.htm

32. Burke, A. (5 Dec. 2017). 10 Facts About American Women in the Workplace. https://www.brookings.edu/blog/brookings-now/2017/12/05/10-facts-about-american-women-in-the-workforce/

33. Warner, J., Corley, D. (21 May 2017). The Women's Leadership Gap: Women's Leadership by the Numbers. Center for American Progress. https://www.americanprogress.org/issues/women/reports/2017/05/21/432758/womens-leadership-gap/

34. Warner, J., Corley, D. (21 May 2017). The Women's Leadership Gap: Women's Leadership by the Numbers. Center for American Progress. https://www.americanprogress.org/issues/women/reports/2017/05/21/432758/womens-leadership-gap/

35. Warner, J., Corley, D. (21 May 2017). The Women's Leadership Gap: Women's Leadership by the Numbers. Center for American Progress. https://www.americanprogress.org/issues/women/reports/2017/05/21/432758/womens-leadership-gap/

36. Warner, J., Corley, D. (21 May 2017). The Women's Leadership Gap: Women's Leadership by the Numbers. Center for American Progress. https://www.americanprogress.org/issues/women/reports/2017/05/21/432758/womens-leadership-gap/

37. Warner, J., Corley, D. (21 May 2017). The Women's Leadership Gap: Women's Leadership by the Numbers. Center for American Progress. https://www.americanprogress.org/issues/women/reports/2017/05/21/432758/womens-leadership-gap/

38. Warner, J., Corley, D. (21 May 2017). The Women's Leadership Gap: Women's Leadership by the Numbers. Center for American Progress. https://www.americanprogress.org/issues/women/reports/2017/05/21/432758/womens-leadership-gap/

39. Warner, J., Corley, D. (21 May 2017). The Women's Leadership Gap: Women's Leadership by the Numbers. Center for American Progress. https://www.americanprogress.org/issues/women/reports/2017/05/21/432758/womens-leadership-gap/

40. Ewing-Nelson, C. (2020). National Women's Law Center. Nearly 2.2 Million Women Have Left the Labor Force Since February. Retrieved January 18, 2021 at https://nwlc.org/wp-content/uploads/2020/11/October-Jobs-Day.pdf

41. Miller, C. (2017). Men and Women Say They're More Different Than Similar. *New York Times*. https://www.nytimes.com/2017/12/05/upshot/men-women-gender-bias-poll.html

42. Warner, J., Corley, D. (21 May 2017). The Women's Leadership Gap: Women's Leadership by the Numbers. Retrieved from https://www.americanprogress.org/issues/women/reports/2017/05/21/432758/womens-leadership-gap/

43. Warner, J., Corley, D. (21 May 2017). The Women's Leadership Gap: Women's Leadership by the Numbers. Retrieved from https://www. americanprogress.org/issues/women/reports/2017/05/21/432758/womens-leadership-gap/

44. Desvaux, G., Devillard, S., Zelicourt, A., Kossoff, C., Labaye, E. and Sancier-Sultan, S. (2017). Women Matter – Time to accelerate. https://www.mckinsey.com/featured-insights/gender-equality/women-matter-ten-years-of-insights-on-gender-diversity

45. Peery, D. (2017). 2019 Survey Report On the Promotion and Retention of Women in Law Firms. https://www.nawl.org/page/2018survey

46. Matias, D. (2019). New Report Says Women Will Soon Be Majority of College-Educated U.S. Workers. NPR. https://www.npr.org/2019/06/20/734408574/new-report-says-college-educated-women-will-soon-make-up-majority-of-u-s-labor-f

47. Duke, S. (2017). The Key to Closing the Gender Gap? Putting More Women in Charge. World Economic Forum. https://www.weforum.org/agenda/2017/11/women-leaders-key-to-workplace-equality/

48. Duke, S. (2017). The Key to Closing the Gender Gap? Putting More Women in Charge. World Economic

Forum. https://www.weforum.org/agenda/2017/11/women-leaders-key-to-workplace-equality/

49. Lagerberg, F. and Schmidt, K. (2020). Women in Business 2020: Putting the Blueprint into Action. Grant Thorton. https://www.grantthornton.global/globalassets/1.-member-firms/global/insights/women-in-business/2020/women-in-business-2020_report.pdf

50. Blomqvist, J. (2020). Finland's Female Leadership Sweep. Korn Ferry. https://www.kornferry.com/insights/articles/finland-women-in-leadership-millennial

51. Blomqvist, J. (2020). Finland's Female Leadership Sweep. Korn Ferry. https://www.kornferry.com/insights/articles/finland-women-in-leadership-millennial

52. Madgavkar, A., Ellingrud, K., and Krishnan, M. (2016). The economic benefits of gender parity. McKinsey & Company. https://www.mckinsey.com/mgi/overview/in-the-news/the-economic-benefits-of- gender-parity

53. Cooney, R. (2005). Taking a New Look – The Enduring Significance of the American Woman Suffrage Movement. Retrieved from https://archive.

mith.umd.edu/womensstudies/ReadingRoom/ History/ Vote/enduring-significance.html

54. Cep, C. (8 July 2019). The Imperfect, Unfinished Work of Women's Suffrage. https://www.newyorker.com/magazine/2019/07/08/the-imperfect-unfinished-work-of-womens-suffrage

55. Cep, C. (8 July 2019). The Imperfect, Unfinished Work of Women's Suffrage. https://www.newyorker.com/magazine/2019/07/08/the-imperfect-unfinished-work-of-womens-suffrage

56. World Economic Forum. (2017). Insight Report: the Global Gender Gap Report. http://www3.weforum.org/docs/WEF_GGGR_2017.pdf

57. Mishra, S. (13 Aug. 2018). Women in the C Suite: The Next Frontier in Gender Diversity. Retrieved from https://corpgov.law.harvard.edu/2018/08/13/women-in-the-C Suite-the-next-frontier-in-gender- diversity/

58. Mishra, S. (13 Aug. 2018). Women in the C Suite: The Next Frontier in Gender Diversity. Retrieved from https://corpgov.law.harvard.edu/2018/08/13/women-in-the-C Suite-the-next-frontier-in-gender- diversity/

59. Gupta, A. (2019). California Companies are Rushing to Find Female Board Members. The New York

Times. (https://www.nytimes.com/2019/12/17/us/california-boardroom-gender-quota.html

60. Blumberg, Y. (2 March 2018). Companies with more female executives make more money – here's why. Retrieved from https://www.cnbc. com/2018/03/02/why-companies-with-female-managers-make-more-money.html

61. Sandberg, D. (2019). When Women Lead, Firms Win. S&P Global. Bureau of Labor Statistics. https://www.spglobal.com/_division_assets/images/special-editorial/iif-2019/whenwomenlead_.pdf

62. Blumberg, Y. (2 March 2018). Companies with more female executives make more money – here's why. Retrieved from https://www.cnbc. com/2018/03/02/why-companies-with-female-managers-make-more-money.html

63. Elsesser, K. (2016). The Truth About Women's Impact on Corporate Boards. Forbes. https://www.forbes.com/sites/kimelsesser/2016/06/23/the-truth-about-womens-impact-on-corporate-boards-its-not-good-news/

64. Committee for Economic Development. (2019). Filling the Pipeline: Advancing More Women Into the C-Suite and on Corporate Boards. https://www.ced.org/reports/filling-the-pipeline-advancing-more-women-into-the-c-suite-and-on-corporate

65. Gurchiek, Kathy. (2019). Top 70 List Highlights Best Companies for Executive Women. Retrieved from https://www.shrm.org/resourcesandtools/hr-topics/behavioral-competencies/global-and-cultural-effectiveness/pages/top-70-list-highlights-best-companies-for-executive-women.aspx

66. Gurchiek, Kathy. (2019). Top 70 List Highlights Best Companies for Executive Women. Retrieved from https://www.shrm.org/resourcesandtools/hr-topics/behavioral-competencies/global-and-cultural-effectiveness/pages/top-70-list-highlights-best-companies-for-executive-women.aspx

67. Gurchiek, Kathy. (2019). Top 70 List Highlights Best Companies for Executive Women. Retrieved from https://www.shrm.org/resourcesandtools/hr-topics/behavioral-competencies/global-and-cultural-effectiveness/pages/top-70-list-highlights-best-companies-for-executive-women.aspx

68. Gurchiek, Kathy. (2019). Top 70 List Highlights Best Companies for Executive Women. Retrieved from https://www.shrm.org/resourcesandtools/hr-topics/behavioral-competencies/global-and-cultural-effectiveness/pages/top-70-list-highlights-best-companies-for-executive-women.aspx

69. Huang, J. Krivkovich, A., Starikova, I., and Zanoschi, D. (2019). Women in the Workplace 2019. Retrieved from https://www. mckinsey.com/featured-insights/gender-equality/women-in-the- workplace-2019

70. Committee for Economic Development. (2019). Filling the Pipeline: Advancing More Women Into the C-Suite and on Corporate Boards. https://www.ced.org/reports/filling-the-pipeline-advancing-more-women-into-the-c-suite-and-on-corporate

71. Warner, J., Corley, D. (2017). The Women's Leadership Gap: Women's Leadership by the Numbers. https://www. americanprogress.org/issues/women/reports/2017/05/21/432758/womens-leadership-gap/

72. Omeokwe, A. (2020). Women Overtake Men as Majority of U.S. Workforce. https://www.wsj.com/articles/women- overtake-men-as-majority-of-u-s-workforce-11578670615

73. Warner, J., Corley, D. (2017). The Women's Leadership Gap: Women's Leadership by the Numbers. https://www. americanprogress.org/issues/women/reports/2017/05/21/432758/womens-leadership-gap/

74. Warner, J., Corley, D. (2017). The Women's Leadership Gap: Women's Leadership by the

Numbers. https://www. americanprogress. org/issues/women/reports/2017/05/21/432758/womens-leadership-gap/

75. Miller, C. (2019). Women Did Everything Right. Then work Got Greedy. The New York Times. https://www.nytimes.com/2019/04/26/upshot/women-long-hours-greedy-professions.html

76. Miller, C. (2019). Women Did Everything Right. Then work Got Greedy. The New York Times. https://www.nytimes.com/2019/04/26/upshot/women-long-hours-greedy-professions.html

77. Cho, R., Kramer, A. (November 2016). Everything You Need to Know about the Equal Pay Act. https://www.icrw.org/wp-content/uploads/2016/11/Everything-You-Need-to-Know-about-the-Equal-Pay-Act.pdf

78. Cho, R., Kramer, A. (November 2016). Everything You Need to Know about the Equal Pay Act. https://www.icrw.org/wp-content/uploads/2016/11/Everything-You-Need-to-Know-about-the-Equal-Pay-Act.pdf

79. Pontefract, D. (10 Jan. 2019). 2020 Hindsight: The CEO Challenge to Fix the Gender Pay Gap. Retrieved from https://www.forbes.com/sites/danpontefract/2019/10/01/2020-hindsight-the-ceo-challenge-to-fix-the-gender-pay-gap/

80. Pontefract, D. (10 Jan. 2019). 2020 Hindsight: The CEO Challenge to Fix the Gender Pay Gap. Retrieved from https://www.forbes.com/sites/danpontefract/2019/10/01/2020-hindsight-the-ceo-challenge-to-fix-the-gender-pay-gap/

81. Payscale. (March 2019). Do Advanced Degrees Help You Get a Higher Salary? The Answer Depends on Your Gender. https://www.payscale.com/career-news/2019/03/do-advanced-degrees-help-you-get-a-higher-salary-the-answer-depends-on-your-gender

82. Gould, E., Schieder, J., and Geier, K. (2016). What is the gender pay gap and is it real? https://www.epi.org/publication/what-is-the-gender-pay-gap-and-is-it-real/

83. Davis, S. (2019). Here is the giant pay disparity between the U.S. Women's National Team winning the World Cup vs. the men. Business Insiders. https://www.businessinsider.com/us-womens-national-team-world-cup-pay-vs-men-2019-7#:~:text=According%20to%20The%20New%20York,for%20the%20Women's%20World%20Cup

84. Kuhl, E. (2020). Gender Pay Gap Contributes to Increased Rates of Depression and Anxiety Among Women. http://www.workplacementalhealth.org/Mental-Health-Topics/Depression/gender-pay-gap-depression-rates

85. Kuhl, E. (2020). Gender Pay Gap Contributes to Increased Rates of Depression and Anxiety Among Women. http://www.workplacementalhealth.org/Mental-Health-Topics/Depression/gender-pay-gap-depression-rates

86. LaFauci, D. (2019). Linkage Publishes New Research on Advancing Women Leaders. Retrieved from https://www.linkageinc.com/leadership-insights/linkage-publishes-new-research-on- advancing-women-leaders/

87. Stevenson, J., Orr, E. (November 2017). We Interviewed 57 Female CEO's to Find Out How More Women Can Get to the Top. https://hbr.org/2017/11/we-interviewed-57-female-ceos-to-find-out-how-more-women-can-get-to-the-top

88. Russell, M., Lepler, L. (May 2017). How We Closed the Gap Between Men's and Women's Retention Rates. Retrieved from https://hbr.org/2017/05/how-we-closed-the-gap-between-mens-and-womens- retention-rates

89. Stevenson, J., Orr, E. (November 2017). We Interviewed 57 Female CEO's to Find Out How More Women Can Get to the Top. https://hbr.org/2017/11/we-interviewed-57-female-ceos-to-find-out-how-more-women-can-get-to-the-top

90. Zalis, S. (28 April 2018). How to Rise the Ranks: Advice from Female Leaders on Making It to the Top. https://www.forbes.com/sites/shelleyzalis/2018/04/28/how-to-rise-the-ranks-advice-from-female-leaders-on-making-it-to-the-top/

91. Zalis, S. (28 April 2018). How to Rise the Ranks: Advice from Female Leaders on Making It to the Top. https://www.forbes.com/sites/shelleyzalis/2018/04/28/how-to-rise-the-ranks-advice-from-female-leaders-on-making-it-to-the-top/

92. Zalis, S. (28 April 2018). How to Rise the Ranks: Advice from Female Leaders on Making It to the Top. https://www.forbes.com/sites/shelleyzalis/2018/04/28/how-to-rise-the-ranks-advice-from-female-leaders-on-making-it-to-the-top/

93. Stevenson, J., Orr, E. (November 2017). We Interviewed 57 Female CEO's to Find Out How More Women Can Get to the Top. https://hbr.org/2017/11/we-interviewed-57-female-ceos-to-find-out-how-more-women-can-get-to-the-top

94. Conant, E. (October 2019). The best and worst countries to be a woman. Retrieved from https://www.nationalgeographic.com/culture/2019/10/peril-progress-prosperity-womens-well-being-around-the-world-feature/

95. Conant, E. (October 2019). The best and worst countries to be a woman. Retrieved from https://www.nationalgeographic.com/culture/2019/10/peril-progress-prosperity-womens-well-being-around-the-world-feature/

96. World Economic Forum. (2020). Global Gender Gap Report 2020. http://www3.weforum.org/docs/WEF_GGGR_2020.pdf

97. Committee for Economic Development. (2019). Filling the Pipeline: Advancing More Women into the C Suite and On Corporate Boards. Retrieved from https://www.ced.org/reports/filling-the- pipeline-advancing-more-women-into-the-C Suite-and-on-corporate

98. Lee, J. (2018). 3 Ways Men Can Help Close the Gender Gap. Entrepreneur. https://www.entrepreneur.com/article/300108

99. Waller, N. (2016). How Men and Women See the Workplace Differently. The Wall Street Journal. http://graphics.wsj.com/how-men-and-women-see-the-workplace-differently/

100. Waller, N. (2016). How Men and Women See the Workplace Differently. The Wall Street Journal. http://graphics.wsj.com/how-men-and-women-see-the-workplace-differently/

101. Carpenter, Julia. (31 Jan. 2018). This is what women have to do to become CEO. CCN Money. https://money.cnn.com/2018/01/31/pf/female-ceos-leadership/index.html

102. Adams, D. (2018). Confessions of a white male CEO. https://www.cuinsight.com/confessions-of-a-white-male-ceo-5-steps-to-inclusive-mentoring.html

103. Mermelshtine, R. (2019). Gender and Inequality in the C Suite. https://good.co/blog/gender-inequality-c-suite/

104. B Mermelshtine, R. (2019). Gender and Inequality in the C Suite. https://good.co/blog/gender-inequality-c-suite/

105. Huang, G. (26 Aug. 2019). New Study Finds Men Want to Help Women at Work, But Just Don't Know How. Forbes. https://www.forbes.com/sites/georgenehuang/2019/08/26/new-study-finds-men-want-to-help-women-at-work-but-just-dont-know-how/

106. Huang, J. Krivkovich, A. Starikova, I., Yee, L., and Zanoschi, D. (30 Sept. 2020). Women in the Workplace 2019. Retrieved from https://www.mckinsey.com/featured-insights/gender-equality/women-in-the- workplace-2019

107. Duckworth, A. (2016). Q & A. https://angeladuckworth.com/qa/

108. Perlis, M. (29 Oct. 2013). 5 Characteristics of Grit—How Many do You Have? https://www.forbes.com/sites/margaretperlis/2013/10/29/5-characteristics-of-grit-what-it-is-why-you-need-it-and-do-you-have-it/

109. Duckworth, Angela. (2016). Grit: The Power of Passion and Perseverance. New York, NY: Scribner.

110. Go Strengths. (2020). What is Grit? Retrieved from gostrengths. com/what-is-grit/

111. Stevenson, J., Orr, E. (November 2017). We Interviewed 57 Female CEO's to Find Out How More Women Can Get to the Top. https://hbr.org/2017/11/we-interviewed-57-female-ceos-to-find-out-how-more-women-can-get-to-the-top

112. Stevenson, J., Orr, E. (November 2017). We Interviewed 57 Female CEO's to Find Out How More Women Can Get to the Top. https://hbr.org/2017/11/we-interviewed-57-female-ceos-to-find-out-how-more-women-can-get-to-the-top

113. Go Strengths. (2020). What is Grit? Retrieved from gostrengths. com/what-is-grit/

114. Hunter, C. (2019). Grit: A Key Ingredient for Leadership, With Insight from Executive Andrew Malek. Retrieved from https://www.einnews.com/pr_news/490552299/

grit-a-key-ingredient-for-leadership-with-insight-from-executive-andrew-malek

115. Maury, R., Stutsman, M. (2019). Women Veterans Are Starting More and More STEM Businesses: Here Are the Resources They Need. Women Entrepreneur. https://www.entrepreneur.com/article/332103

116. The Committee on House Administration of the U.S. House of Representatives. (2006). Women in Congress 1917-2006. https://www.govinfo.gov/content/pkg/GPO-CDOC-108hdoc223/pdf/GPO-CDOC-108hdoc223.pdf

117. Crow, M., Dabars, W.B. (2015). Designing the new American University. Baltimore, Md. Johns Hopkins University Press.

118. History, Art & Archives; United States House of Representatives. (2019). The Year of the Woman, 1848-1920. https://history.house.gov/Exhibitions-and-Publications/WIC/Historical-Essays/No-Lady/Womens-Rights/

119. Weiss, E. (May 2018). Women's Movements are Facing Internal Divisions. History Shows That's Not Necessarily a Bad thing. https://time.com/5186987/womens-movement-disagreement/

120. Horowitz, J., Igielinik, R., and Parker, K. (20 Sept. 2018). Women and Leadership 2018. https://www.pewsocialtrends.org/2018/09/20/women-and-leadership-2018/

121. Desilver, D. (18 Dec. 2018). A record number of women will be serving in the new Congress. Retrieved from https://www.pewresearch.org/fact-tank/2018/12/18/record-number-women-in-congress/).

122. Layton, R. (29 June 2019). Hundreds of Women Have Lead Roles in the Trump Administration. 45 More Await Senate Confirmation. Retrieved from https://www.forbes.com/sites/roslynlayton/2019/06/29/hundreds-of-women-have-lead-roles-in-the-trump-administration-45-more-await-senate-confirmation/#7ab41c37250e

123. Abbott, K., Mohapatra. (2019). How Business Can Build a 'Future of Work' That works for women. Business for Social Responsibility (BSR). https://www.bsr.org/en/our-insights/report-view/future-of-work-womens-economic-empowerment

124. Abbott, K., Mohapatra. (2019). How Business Can Build a 'Future of Work' That works for women. Business for Social Responsibility (BSR). https://www.bsr.org/en/our-insights/report-view/future-of-work-womens-economic-empowerment

125. Madgavkar, A., Manyika, J., Krishnan, M., et.al. (2019). The future of women at work: Transitions in the age of automation. McKinsey & Company. https://www.mckinsey.com/featured-insights/gender-equality/the-future-of-women-at-work-transitions-in-the-age-of-automation

126. Madgavkar, A., Manyika, J., Krishnan, M., et.al. (2019). The future of women at work: Transitions in the age of automation. McKinsey & Company. https://www.mckinsey.com/featured-insights/gender-equality/the-future-of-women-at-work-transitions-in-the-age-of-automation

127. Kinder, M. (2019). The Future of Work for Women: Technology, Automation & the Overlooked Workforce. Retrieved from https://www.newamerica.org/work-workers-technology/shiftlabs/blog/future-work-women/

128. Lorenzo, R., Voigt, N., Tsusaka, M., Krentz, M., and Abouzahr, K. (2018). How Diverse Leadership Teams Boost Innovation. https://www.bcg.com/publications/2018/how-diverse-leadership-teams-boost-innovation

129. Madgavkar, A., Ellingrud, K., and Krishnan, M. (2016). The economic benefits of gender parity. McKinsey & Company. https://

www. mckinsey.com/mgi/overview/in-the-news/the-economic-benefits-of- gender-parity

130. Abbott, K., Mohapatra. (2019). How Business Can Build a 'Future of Work' That works for women. Business for Social Responsibility (BSR). https://www.bsr.org/en/our-insights/report-view/future-of-work-womens-economic-empowerment

131. Business Roundtable. (2019). Business Roundtable Redefines the Purpose of a Corporation to Promote' An Economy That Serves All Americans'. https://www.businessroundtable.org/business-roundtable-redefines-the-purpose-of-a-corporation-to-promote-an-economy-that-serves-all-americans

132. Business Roundtable. (2019). Business Roundtable Redefines the Purpose of a Corporation to Promote' An Economy That Serves All Americans'. https://www.businessroundtable.org/business-roundtable-redefines-the-purpose-of-a-corporation-to-promote-an-economy-that-serves-all-americans

133. Business Roundtable. (2019). Business Roundtable Redefines the Purpose of a Corporation to Promote' An Economy That Serves All Americans'. https://www.businessroundtable.org/business-roundtable-redefines-the-purpose-of-a-corporation-to-promote-an-economy-that-serves-all-americans

134. Business Roundtable. (2019). Business Roundtable Redefines the Purpose of a Corporation to Promote' An Economy That Serves All Americans'. https://www.businessroundtable.org/business-roundtable-redefines-the-purpose-of-a-corporation-to-promote-an-economy-that-serves-all-americans

135. Business Roundtable. (2019). Business Roundtable Redefines the Purpose of a Corporation to Promote' An Economy That Serves All Americans'. https://www.businessroundtable.org/business-roundtable-redefines-the-purpose-of-a-corporation-to-promote-an-economy-that-serves-all-americans

136. Desvaux, G., Devillard, S., Zelicourt, A., Kossoff, C., Labaye, E. and Sancier-Sultan, S. (2017). Women Matter – Time to accelerate. https://www.mckinsey.com/featured-insights/gender-equality/women-matter-ten-years-of-insights-on-gender-diversity

137. U.S. News & World Report. (2020). Power: these countries project their influence on the world stage. Retrieved from https:// www.usnews.com/news/best-countries/power-rankings

138. Ward, K. (2011). The world in 2050: Quantifying the shift in the global economy. https://warwick.ac.uk/fac/soc/pais/research/researchcentres/csgr/green/foresight/

economy/2011_hsbc_the_world_in_2050_-_quantifying_the_shift_in_the_global_economy.pdf

139. Ward, K. (2011). The world in 2050: Quantifying the shift in the global economy. https://warwick.ac.uk/fac/soc/pais/research/researchcentres/csgr/green/foresight/economy/2011_hsbc_the_world_in_2050_-_quantifying_the_shift_in_the_global_economy.pdf

140. Blair, C. (2016). Empowering Women Will Drive Economic Growth. https://www.cfr.org/blog/empowering-women-will-drive-economic-growth

141. Jagannathan, M. (27 June 2019). Do you want to be CEO? Women face these extra obstacles on their way to the C Suite. https://www.marketwatch.com/story/do-you-want-to-be-ceo-your-chances-are-much-better-if-youre-a-man-2019-06-27

142. Jagannathan, M. (27 June 2019). Do you want to be CEO? Women face these extra obstacles on their way to the C Suite. https://www.marketwatch.com/story/do-you-want-to-be-ceo-your-chances-are-much-better-if-youre-a-man-2019-06-27

143. Murphy, B. (2016). 5 Essential Traits of Leaders with True Grit. https://www.inc.com/bill-murphy-jr/do-you-really-have-grit-or-are-you-just-a-stubborn-jerk.html

144. Goleman, D. (January 2013). The Focused Leader. Harvard Business Review. https://hbr.org/2004/01/what-makes-a-leader

145. Goleman, D. (January 2013). The Focused Leader. Harvard Business Review. https://hbr.org/2004/01/what-makes-a-leader

146. Goleman, D. (January 2013). The Focused Leader. Harvard Business Review. https://hbr.org/2004/01/what-makes-a-leader

147. Goleman, D. (January 2013). The Focused Leader. Harvard Business Review. https://hbr.org/2004/01/what-makes-a-leader

148. Case, J. (2019). Most every successful person has a story of excruciating failure in their past – and for good reason. https://www.businessinsider.com/success-failure-ceo-jean-case-2019-1

149. Case, J. (2019). Most every successful person has a story of excruciating failure in their past – and for good reason. https://www.businessinsider.com/success-failure-ceo-jean-case-2019-1

150. Williams, M. (2017). John Dewey in the 21st Century. Journal of Inquiry & Action in Education 9(1).

151. Morrissey, M. (6 Dec. 2016). The Power of Writing Down Your Goals and Dreams.

Retrieved from https://www.huffpost.com/entry/the- power-of-writing-down_b_12002348

152. Deloitte. (2018). The symphonic C Suite: teams leading teams. https://www2.deloitte.com/us/en/insights/focus/human-capital-trends/2018/senior-leadership-c-suite-collaboration.html

153. Deloitte. (2018). The symphonic C Suite: teams leading teams. https://www2.deloitte.com/us/en/insights/focus/human-capital-trends/2018/senior-leadership-c-suite-collaboration.html

154. Porter, M., Nohria, N. (2018). The Leader's Calendar. Harvard Business Review - August 2018 USA

155. Porter, M., Nohria, N. (2018). The Leader's Calendar. Harvard Business Review - August 2018 USA

156. Patel, S. (18 Aug. 2016). Daily Routines of Fortune 500 Leaders (And what you can learn from them. Retrieved from https://www.startups. com/library/expert-advice/how-fortune-500-leaders-schedule-their- days

157. Pruitt, J. (2017). 5 Performance Indicators Every CEO Should be Tracking. www.inc.com/jeff-pruitt/5-performance-indicators-every-ceo-should-be-tracking.html

158. Botelho, E. Powell, K., Kincaid, S., and Wang, D. (May 2017). What Sets Successful CEOs Apart? https://

store.hbr.org/product/what-sets-successful-ceos-apart/R1703C

159. Stevenson, J., Crandell, S. (2017). Women CEOs Speak. Korn Ferry Institute. https://engage.kornferry.com/Global/FileLib/Women_CEOs_speak/KFI_Rockefeller_Study_Women_CEOs_Speak.pdf

160. Stevenson, J., Crandell, S. (2017). Women CEOs Speak. Korn Ferry Institute. https://engage.kornferry.com/Global/FileLib/Women_CEOs_speak/KFI_Rockefeller_Study_Women_CEOs_Speak.pdf

161. Sweeten-Schults, L. (October 2019). Panel of Women Business Leaders Sets the Pace. https://news.gcu.edu/2019/10/grand-canyon-university-women-business-leaders-set-the-pace-unapologetically/

162. Botelho, E. Powell, K., Kincaid, S., and Wang, D. (May 2017). What Sets Successful CEOs Apart? https://store.hbr.org/product/what-sets-successful-ceos-apart/R1703C

163. Stevenson, J., Crandell, S. (2017). Women CEOs Speak. Korn Ferry Institute. https://engage.kornferry.com/Global/FileLib/Women_CEOs_speak/KFI_Rockefeller_Study_Women_CEOs_Speak.pdf

164. Morad, R. (2019). How Gender is a growth engine for the global economy. Retrieved from https://www.

nbcnews.com/know- your-value/feature/how-gen-der-equality-growth-engine-global- economy-nc-na963591

165. Morad, R. (2019). How Gender is a growth engine for the global economy. Retrieved from https://www.nbcnews.com/know- your-value/feature/how-gender-equality-growth-engine-global- economy-ncna963591

166. Fortune Knowledge Group & Royal Bank of Canada. (2017). www.rbc.com/newsroom/news/2017/20170307-fortune.html

167. Fortune Knowledge Group & Royal Bank of Canada. (2017). www.rbc.com/newsroom/news/2017/20170307-fortune.html

168. Peluso, M., Baird, C., and Kesterson-Townes, L. (2019). Women, leadership and the priority paradox. Retrieved from https:// www.ibm.com/downloads/cas/YZWEXLPG

169. Peluso, M., Baird, C., and Kesterson-Townes, L. (2019). Women, leadership and the priority paradox. Retrieved from https:// www.ibm.com/downloads/cas/YZWEXLPG

170. Peluso, M., Baird, C., and Kesterson-Townes, L. (2019). Women, leadership and the priority paradox.

Retrieved from https:// www.ibm.com/downloads/cas/ YZWEXLPG

171. Tsusaka, M., Greiser, C., Krentz, M., and Reeves, M. (2019). Winning the '20s: The Business Imperative for Diversity. https://bcghendersoninstitute.com/winning-the-20s-achieving-innovation-resilience-through-diversity-e2cc98a97c07

172. Huang, J. Krivkovich, A. Starikova, I., Yee, L., and Zanoschi, D. (30 Sept. 2020). Women in the Workplace 2019. Retrieved from https://www.mckinsey.com/featured-insights/gender-equality/women-in-the-workplace-2019

173. Tsusaka, M., Greiser, C., Krentz, M., and Reeves, M. (2019). Winning the '20s: The Business Imperative for Diversity. https://bcghendersoninstitute.com/winning-the-20s-achieving-innovation-resilience-through-diversity-e2cc98a97c07

174. Lorenzo, R., Voigt, N., Tsusaka, M., Krentz, M., and Abouzahr, K. (2018). How Diverse Leadership Teams Boost Innovation. https://www.bcg.com/publications/2018/how-diverse-leadership-teams-boost-innovation

175. Lorenzo, R., Voigt, N., Tsusaka, M., Krentz, M., and Abouzahr, K. (2018). How Diverse Leadership Teams Boost Innovation.

https://www.bcg.com/publications/2018/how-diverse-leadership-teams-boost-innovation

176. Lorenzo, R., Voigt, N., Tsusaka, M., Krentz, M., and Abouzahr, K. (2018). How Diverse Leadership Teams Boost Innovation. https://www.bcg.com/publications/2018/how-diverse-leadership-teams-boost-innovation

177. Lorenzo, R., Voigt, N., Tsusaka, M., Krentz, M., and Abouzahr, K. (2018). How Diverse Leadership Teams Boost Innovation. https://www.bcg.com/publications/2018/how-diverse-leadership-teams-boost-innovation

178. Lorenzo, R., Voigt, N., Tsusaka, M., Krentz, M., and Abouzahr, K. (2018). How Diverse Leadership Teams Boost Innovation. https://www.bcg.com/publications/2018/how-diverse-leadership-teams-boost-innovation

179. Lee, T., Duckworth, A. (September 2018). Organizational Grit. Retrieved from https://hbr.org/2018/09/organizational-grit

180. Duckworth, A. (September 2018). Organizational Grit. Retrieved from https://hbr.org/2018/09/organizational-grit

181. Chira, S. (21 July 2017). Why Women Aren't CEOs, According to Women Who Almost Were. Retrieved from https://www.nytimes. com/2017/07/21/sunday-review/women-ceos-glass-ceiling.html

182. Tsusaka, M., Greiser, C., Krentz, M., and Reeves, M. (2019). Winning the '20s: The Business Imperative for Diversity. https://bcghendersoninstitute.com/winning-the-20s-achieving-innovation-resilience-through-diversity-e2cc98a97c07

183. LaFauci, D. (2019). Linkage Publishes New Research on Advancing Women Leaders. Retrieved from https://www.linkageinc. com/leadership-insights/linkage-publishes-new-research-on- advancing-women-leaders/

184. SAS. (2020). Predictive Analytics: What it is and why it matters. SAS. www.sas.com/en_us/insights/analytics/predictive-analytics.html

185. Lee, E. (11 Jan. 2020). Her A.I. Analyzes Your Performance Review for Gender Bias. Retrieved from https://www.ozy.com/the-new-and-the-next/her-ai-analyzes-your-performance-review-for-gender-bias/259605/

186. Lee, E. (11 Jan. 2020). Her A.I. Analyzes Your Performance Review for Gender Bias. Retrieved from https://www.ozy.com/the-new-and-the-next/

her-ai-analyzes-your-performance-review-for-gender-bias/259605/

187. Lee, E. (11 Jan. 2020). Her A.I. Analyzes Your Performance Review for Gender Bias. Retrieved from https://www.ozy.com/the-new-and-the-next/her-ai-analyzes-your-performance-review-for-gender-bias/259605/

188. Campbell, J., DeBlois, P., and Oblinger, D. (July 2007). Academic Analytics: A New Tool for a New Era. Retrieved from https:// er.educause.edu/articles/2007/7/academic-analytics-a-new-tool-for-a- new-era

189. Campbell, J., DeBlois, P., and Oblinger, D. (July 2007). Academic Analytics: A New Tool for a New Era. Retrieved from https:// er.educause.edu/articles/2007/7/academic-analytics-a-new-tool-for-a- new-era

190. Charan, R. (22 Jan. 2015). The algorithmic CEO. Fortune. https://fortune.com/2015/01/22/the-algorithmic-ceo/

191. Diversity Best Practices. (2017). Diversity Best Practices Research Report: Developing Next Generation of Women Leaders. https://www. www.diversitybestpractices.com/research-report-building-an-age-inclusive-culture-and-embedding-age-as-diversity-dimensionresearch

192. Coates, M. (2018). 5 Factors to Make Your Corporate Culture Effective. https://www.theglobeandmail.com/report-on-business/careers/leadership-lab/five-factors-to-make-your-corporate-culture-effective/article20008618/#:~:text=Follow%20topics%20related%20to%20this,Organizational%20culture%20Follow

193. Coy, C. (4 May 2017). Four Ways Company Culture Can Support Women in Leadership. Retrieved from https://www.cornerstoneondemand.com/rework/four-ways-company-culture-can- support-women-leadership

194. Coy, C. (4 May 2017). Four Ways Company Culture Can Support Women in Leadership. Retrieved from https://www.cornerstoneondemand.com/rework/four-ways-company-culture-can- support-women-leadership

195. Elsesser, K. (2019). New LeanIn Study: The Broken Rung Keeping Women from Managemen. Forbes. https://www.forbes.com/sites/kimelsesser/2019/10/15/new-leanin-study-the-broken-rung-keeping-women-from-management/?sh=4a8b43747803

196. Elsesser, K. (2019). New LeanIn Study: The Broken Rung Keeping Women from Managemen. Forbes. https://www.forbes.com/sites/kimelsesser/2019/10/15/new-leanin-study-the-broken-rung-keeping-women-from-management/?sh=4a8b43747803

197. Elsesser, K. (2019). New LeanIn Study: The Broken Rung Keeping Women from Managemen. Forbes. https://www.forbes.com/sites/kimelsesser/2019/10/15/new-leanin-study-the-broken-rung-keeping-women-from-management/?sh=4a8b43747803

198. Lankford, J. (2019). How growth-minded CEOs operate their talent management systems. Retrieved from https://biztimes.com/how-growth-minded-ceos-operate-their-talent-management- systems/

199. LaFauci, D. (2019). Linkage Publishes New Research on Advancing Women Leaders. Retrieved from https://www.linkageinc.com/leadership-insights/linkage-publishes-new-research-on- advancing-women-leaders/

200. Cautela, D. (2019). Three Ways to Promote Gender Diversity in the C Suite. LinkedIn. https://business.linkedin.com/talent-solutions/blog/talent-leadership/2019/3-ways-to-promote-gender-diversity-in-the-c-suite-

201. McGregor, J. (9 Jan. 2019). Nearly three-quarters of executives pick proteges who look just like them. The Washington Post. https://www.washingtonpost.com/business/2019/01/09/nearly-three-quarters-executives-pick-proteges-who-look-just-like-them/

202. McGregor, J. (9 Jan. 2019). Nearly three-quarters of executives pick proteges who look just like them. The

Washington Post. https://www.washingtonpost.com/business/2019/01/09/nearly-three-quarters-executives-pick-proteges-who-look-just-like-them/

203. Rissman, G. (2019). Pushing Companies to Improve on Gender Equity. Retrieved from https://www.asyousow.org/blog/2019/3/19/pushing-companies-improve-gender-equality

204. Gilliland, N. (2020). How bands are fighting against gender stereotypes. Econsultancy. https://econsultancy.com/how-brands-are-fighting-against-gender-stereotypes/

205. Coffman, K., Flikkema, C., and Shurchkov, O. (2019). Gender Stereotypes in Deliberation and Team Decisions. Harvard Business School. https://hbswk.hbs.edu/item/gender-stereotypes-in-deliberation-and-team-decisions

206. Committee for Economic Development. (2019). Filling the Pipeline: Advancing More Women Into the C-Suite and on Corporate Boards. https://www.ced.org/reports/filling-the-pipeline-advancing-more-women-into-the-c-suite-and-on-corporate

207. Thomas, D., Gabarro, J. (1999). Breaking Through. Retrieved from https://www.amazon.com/Breaking-Through-Minority-Executives-Corporate/dp/0875848664

208. Robinson, S. (2020). Best 100 Companies for Women's Leadership Development. Diversity Woman Media. https://www.diversitywoman.com/best-100-companies-for-womens-leadership-development/

209. Robinson, S. (2020). Best 100 Companies for Women's Leadership Development. Diversity Woman Media. https://www.diversitywoman.com/best-100-companies-for-womens-leadership-development/

210. ASEAN (Association of Southeast Asian Nations). (2015). ASEAN 2025: Forging Ahead Together. ASEAN Communities. https://www.asean.org/storage/2015/12/ASEAN-2025-Forging-Ahead-Together-final.pdf

211. Washington State University. (2020). More Women Are Joining the C-Suite. Here's How They're Doing It. https://moderonlinemba.wsu.edu/blog/more-women-are-joining-the-c-suite-heres-how-theyre-doing-it/

212. Modern Diplomacy. (2019). Women in leadership bring better business performance. https://moderndiplomacy.eu/2019/05/25/women-in-leadership-bring-better-business-performance/

213. Ryan, J. (2020). Here's How to Propel More Women into the C-Suite. Center for Creative Leadership. https://www.ccl.

org/articles/linkedin-influencer-columns/heres-propel-women-c-suite/

214. Fortune Knowledge Group & Royal Bank of Canada. (2017). www.rbc.com/newsroom/news/2017/20170307-fortune.html

CPSIA information can be obtained
at www.ICGtesting.com
Printed in the USA
BVHW042120030222
628054BV00019B/339